WINNING
THE
GREATEST
GAME OF ALL

"THE NEW ERA IN MULTI-LEVEL MARKETING"

WRITTEN BY
RANDY WARD

D0288144

A Multi-level Marketing Handbook for
the Coaches and the Players:

- **RECRUITING**
- **TRAINING**
- **MOTIVATING**
- **WINNING**
- **CONTRIBUTING**

CIMARRON
MANAGEMENT
CORPORATION

FIRST PRINTING ...... SEPTEMBER 1984
SECOND PRINTING ..... MARCH 1985
THIRD PRINTING ...... APRIL 1987
FOURTH PRINTING ...... APRIL 1989
FIFTH PRINTING ...... MAY 1990
SIXTH PRINTING ...... JULY 1991

Library of Congress Catalog Card Number: 84-72262
PRINTED IN THE UNITED STATES OF AMERICA

ISBN: (HARDBOUND) 0-9613958-0-X
(SOFTBOUND) 0-9613958-1-8

Published by
CIMARRON MANAGEMENT CORPORATION
CIMARRON PUBLISHING COMPANY
333 American Way, Jennings, OK 74038-0159
(918) 757-2235

DEDICATED TO
MY CHILDREN

Randy Joe Ward, II
Cherami Chantel Ward
Jeremy Kalon Ward

ACKNOWLEDGEMENTS:

This book, like most, is a synthesis of past experiences and relationships. And to all of them I am deeply grateful.

There are persons who have contributed directly to this project and they deserve individual recognition. Initially, I want to thank my parents, for without them I wouldn't be. Their support and love have always been evident and has always made a big difference in my life. My children have allowed me to devote a lot of time and energy to my business. Without their support I would not have had the experiences which led to this book.

It would not have been possible to meet our production schedule if it were not for my sister, Sandra Patton, and our Compaq Plus computer. Sandra, her husband, Paul, and the computer worked weekends and late nights in order to meet our time requirements.

I owe a debt of gratitude to the industries in which I have received my business experience. My special thanks go out to the publishing, insurance, real estate, and direct selling industries. Then there are all of the wonderful people who have been associates in my various projects and businesses. Those who have come and gone are especially important, since they are the ones who inspired me to look at the possibility of narrowing the gap between recruiting a person and keeping them in the business. I sincerely thank all of you who have shared some of your life with me.

Many of the breakthrough qualities of this book were made possible by my participation in the training programs offered by various companies. Their workshops and seminars have enabled me to understand the power available to anyone who will operate within the framework of Contribution, Commitment and Integrity.

And finally, a very special thanks to Larry Mullins, who himself is an author, an artist and the president of Actionizing, Inc., a company devoted to human development. Larry contributed greatly to this book's quality through illustration and production supervision.

CONTENTS:

1.

THE GAME OF LIFE versus THE ACCELERATED GAME OF LIFE 19

TRIPLE BREAKTHROUGH: THE NEW MLM/THE NEW YOU/BE COACHABLE/ COME FROM CONTRIBUTION AND GET WHAT YOU GIVE.

2.
THE RULES OF
THE GAME 39

MLM UNIVERSITY: EMOTIONAL GIANT/
INVESTMENT/DUPLICATION/PRODUCT
MOVEMENT/WIDTH versus DEPTH/
CONTRIBUTION/PERSONAL GROWTH.

3.
A PLAYER'S
NATURAL
PROGRESSION 59

STAGES OF PROGRESS: FORMULATIVE
(DESIGNING YOUR MLM FUTURE)/
CONCENTRATION (BUILDING YOUR MLM
FOUNDATION)/MOMENTUM (YOUR MLM
ORGANIZATION TAKES SHAPE)/
STABILITY (PERSONAL SATISFACTION
AND FINANCIAL INDEPENDENCE).

4.
ESTABLISHING
A GAME PLAN 71

THE PATH: TAKE A STAND/WHICH MLM
COMPANY/KNOW AND USE PRODUCTS/
SPONSOR 3 × 3/WEEKLY FORUMS/ PURPOSE.

5.

THE SCOREBOARD 117

THE SCORE: BE ORGANIZED/KEEP
RECORDS/MAILING LIST/PHONE TREE/
HANGING FILES/VOLUME AND BONUS
RECORDS.

6.

THE NEW ERA

IN MULTI-LEVEL

MARKETING 141

THE NEW ERA: THE 100TH MONKEY/IT'S
NOT THE LEARNING BUT THE DOING/
PROBLEMS/PLAY FULL-OUT WITH
COMMITMENT.

APPENDIX

NETWORK TRAINING 151

NOT THE END:
BUT THE BEGINNING/ONGOING
SUPPORT/MONTHLY PLAYS.

INTRODUCTION

Here is a book that will shake your mind, brush the dust from between your ears, and nourish you with fresh ideas for packing your life with more adventure, love and wealth than you ever thought possible!

Do you know the difference between those who are merely surviving and those who are winning the prizes of life? Is the person making $200,000 a year 10 times better than the one earning $20,000?

Of course not! Only small differences separate them. But those differences seem to be the best kept secrets of success. But not any more! Randy Ward will tell you exactly what those differences are. Not only that, he will help you be one of those magnificent people who makes a difference, with his or her life!

How did he discover those unique qualities that can turn every day into a winning game? He did it! He became a winner in every task he tackled.

But Randy is different than most winners who tell you they got there by talent, hard work or luck. Randy's genius is the ability to perceive certain specific processes and steps underlying his, and any other, outstanding achievements.

And those strategies can be learned and put to work immediately by any individual who wants a bigger slice of life!

If you are determined to be all that you can be, then start by reading this book!

> **BOB CONKLIN**
>
> **Chairman of the Board
> Conklin Company, Inc.**

"I believe that the universe was set up to honor any and all clearly defined intentions backed by absolute commitment."

Randy Ward

FOREWARD

WINNING THE GREATEST GAME OF ALL is a unique book in many respects. Not only does it have the divinity of simplicity in its presentation of fundamental and helpful ideas, but the entire content is digestible and enjoyable.

You will rarely find such a combination of workable principles illustrated through humorous cartoons and convincing examples.

I can say without fear of contradiction that this book will take its rightful place among the great books of our time.

CAVETT ROBERT
The National Speaker's Association

PREFACE

The purpose of this book is to be the best recruiting, training and motivational tool ever available to multi-level marketing distributors. It is unique in that it combines these key aspects of the MLM business. Its power comes from straight talk and the hard hitting appeal of its sports language. Finally, the rules are made clear and duplicatable, and a step-by-step game plan is offered. It becomes clear what you are up against, what is required of you and the potential rewards. After reading this book, you will be able to make a quality decision as to whether you want to be a participant or spectator, whether you want to play or sit on the side lines?

Sure, if you play, you are apt to be injured. But I assure you, it's much more exciting and fulfilling to play the game than to merely watch it.

The "accelerated game of life," yeah it's tough, but the coaching of this book can get you through the trying times. And most importantly, the ongoing support of our Total Network Training Program, can keep your "winning edge" sharp and keep you in the game.

After all, most people fail at the "game of life," because they are not even in the game. This book has a tendency to throw you in the ring with the confidence and equipment necessary to become a champion.

WINNIN

THE GREATES

G

GAME OF ALL

1

THE GAME OF LIFE
versus
THE ACCELERATED
GAME OF LIFE

As I sit here in the sunshine, mid-July, I am thinking of you as my teammate in the greatest game of all, the game of life. My own insatiable desire to learn, to be and to have, has accelerated me quite rapidly into a coaching position. As we work together, let's strive to maintain the empowering relationship of coach and player.

Several years ago, it became quite clear that the more willing a person is to be coached, the quicker and easier he will achieve success. Since that time, I have been coached to success in the businesses of insurance and real estate, as well as, land development, construction and oil. After learning the rules of a particular business, formulating a game plan and being coached to success, the challenge was gone. I would then repeat the process in a different business venture.

The "game of survival" and the "money game" were extremely challenging, until oil and gas exploration pushed our net worth to over a million dollars in 1981. By 1983, I was searching for a new challenge, a new meaning. The financial security met a need, but didn't have anything to do with happiness, peace-of-mind and fulfillment. We have all heard that money can't buy happiness, and suddenly I found myself confronted with that harsh reality. I was confronted with the fact that all of us have a deeprooted desire to believe our lives make a difference. You and I both want to know that we have lived and played the game, and have made a contribution to life.

Even though the desire to contribute is basic to our natures, it rarely becomes a driving force in our lives - as long as we are playing the "survival game." After getting survival handled, the natural tendency is a desire to "save the world," so to speak.

Consequently, I was continually confronted with drives like:

- *having peace of mind and assisting others in experiencing the same.*
- *having empowering relationships with family and friends and empowering others to do likewise.*
- *being loved unconditionally and being able to love others in that capacity.*
- *being accepted the way I am and returning the same consideration.*
- *having a freedom to do what I want to do and enhancing the freedom of others.*
- *being a "high-performance" person and a spark which motivates others.*
- *maintaining good health and being an example for others.*
- *experiencing my own magnificence and inspiring others to experience their own.*
- *and so forth.*

since the world has always had a much greater effect on me than I have had on it, the task seemed overwhelming. How was I going to save the world, while leading a pleasant life? Sound familiar?

WINNING THE GREATEST GAME OF ALL

The first step is to accept the fact that the world doesn't need to be saved, and even if it did, it wouldn't be your responsibility. Your main responsibility, as a teammate in the "game of life," is to "play full-out" and promote teamwork. Spencer Hays, President of the Southwestern Publishing Company of Nashville, used to say, "Do your best and don't sweat the rest."

Coming to grips with the fact that we are all teammates, and all have important positions to play, it becomes clear that anytime we make a positive difference in an individual's life, it affects the entire team. In other words, we can make a difference in the world by helping one person.

As the search continued for a challenging vehicle through which to experience fulfillment, it became clear that it was not, and could never be, a job or business. The vehicle can only be life itself! The "game of life" is where we fulfill our inherent needs of acceptance, love, relationships, health, freedom and "making a difference."

Even though the "survival game" and "money game" are aspects of the "game of life," most of our teammates are slaves to them, without the freedom to play the big game. It's sort of like wanting to play Major League baseball and only being old enough to play Little League.

So here we are - all of us wanting and needing to play the "game of life" but being forced to play the "survival game." NO CHOICE! TOO BAD!

But wait! Maybe there is a choice. Wouldn't it be great to play the "game of life" and get paid for it? Wouldn't it be great to earn while we learn? Wouldn't it be great to discover an accelerated course in the fulfillment of life?

In May of 1983, one of our oil partners, Terrel Gipson, introduced me to the "accelerated game of life." It has been around for a long time, yet very few people have recognized it for what it really is. And as far as I know, its real significance has never been expressed.

THE NORMAL GAME
versus
THE ACCELERATED GAME

The "normal game of life" is where the majority of our teammates are, and it is merely the path of least resistance. The game contains most of the elements - such as, relationships, personal growth, the "money game," the opportunity to make a difference, etc. But the accelerated game provides the opportunity to develop your skills more quickly. It is a way to speed up the process of personal growth, a much more direct path to friends, wealth, travel and "making a difference."

The "accelerated game of life" is not for everyone. It is "hardball," and I contend that many people have failed at it because they never knew the rules. They were trying to play hardball with softball rules. Of course, they got slaughtered.

Since I'm not into leading sheep to the slaughter, my intention is to provide you with what is needed to play and win. A good

23

coach would never send you into a football game without telling you what to expect, and without providing you with protective equipment. By the same token, I want you to enter the "accelerated game of life" knowing what you are up against, knowing the rules and having a step-by-step proven game plan.

As a coach, you must talk straight, tell it like it is! You must know what you are up against, what the rules are and the potential rewards. Only then can you make a quality decision to play or watch. As a hardball coach, one cannot spend time with those who want to play soft-ball. No matter how skilled we are, and no matter how well-coached, we cannot win the accelerated game playing by the normal rules.

The value and rewards of playing the accelerated game cannot be overemphasized. It's like playing PAC-MAN for keys instead of cherries. Everything is faster, the points are higher, and we are apt to achieve a more satisfying score. If we never get beyond the cherries, we will not even be in the same league as those who play for keys.

THE ACCELERATED GAME DEFINED

So, what is the "accelerated game of life"? The accelerated game is a vehicle through which we can fulfill our needs more quickly. The vehicle is the popular, but misunderstood, business of multi-level marketing. (MLM will be used to abbreviate multi-level marketing.)

I hesitate to even refer to MLM as a business. Yes, it is a business, but it is much more than that. Some refer to it as a way of life; but it is even more than that. It is life! It is life accelerated! The fact that it is also a business enables us to "earn while we learn." It enables us to earn a living while we learn the most important lessons of life.

Once you recognize MLM for what it really is, you will be able to use it as a "rapid transit" vehicle. It can shorten the time between now and your desired destination, like a commercial jet can move you across the U. S. faster than a train.

So, we now have a new definition for multi-level marketing. MLM is the "accelerated game of life." With this in mind, let's see what your needs and desires are, and the important role MLM can play in their acquisition.

It is my contention that MLM is like an airplane which can speed you to whatever you want in life. We could say that most people have never been taught how to pilot this vehicle. As a result, 85% of those climbing in the cockpit crash and burn. There needs to be an instructor pilot (coach) who can keep the airplane in the air long enough for the student to "get the hang of it." Later chapters will coach you in the skills of flying. You will learn how to fly high and fast, safely above the masses of land rovers. You will learn the rules of the game and be coached into "stardom."

But for now, let's take a look at how MLM speeds up the process. Surveys have indicated that the following needs and desires emerge for most people. To be simple and brief, I shall lump them into three categories: SUR-VIVAL, ESTHETIC, CONTRIBUTION.

I. SURVIVAL NEEDS: These needs are the most basic and contain all of the money needs. Until we handle food, shelter and clothing, it is difficult to assume a more important position on the team. In this category we find:

1. **THE NEED TO BE BOSS:** We all have this desire, because it offers flexibility and a sense of accomplishment and responsibility.

2. **THE NEED TO EARN WHILE WE LEARN:** Many people are trapped in "dead end" jobs because their paycheck means survival.

3. **THE NEED TO DEVELOP COMMUNI-CATIVE SKILLS:** It has been said that 70%

of our results in life are directly proportional to how well we communicate.

4. **THE NEED FOR FINANCIAL INDEPENDENCE:** It is obvious that only through financial independence can we graduate from the "survival game."

5. **THE NEED TO BE HEALTHY:** Basic to life itself is the cliche, "survival of the fittest." The cold hard fact is, that the healthier and more adaptable we are, the better our performance will be. They say that "health is wealth," and must be valid because, as a rule, successful people are healthier than those who are not.

We could list many other specific, survival-type needs. Here we are talking about the financial freedom to experience life outside of the "survival game."

Most all of us know, or know of, someone who has achieved a level of financial independence and a lifestyle through MLM, which other occupations rarely produce. The accompanying lifestyle is unique because, in MLM, you are not a slave to overhead, employees, suppliers and clients. The duplication principle in MLM allows for unlimited financial rewards. "The sky's the limit." Unlike other businesses, whose natural tendency is contraction, the natural tendency in MLM is expansion. For example, from the day we began producing a new oil well, the potential income has continually declined. The reserves are being depleted. From the initial base of a MLM organization, you can experience quite rapid expansion. The income potential is great,

DECLINING PRODUCTION AT WORK!

but you must be willing to pay the price. You must be willing to learn the rules, develop a sense of true purpose and play full-out. For those of you who do, truly, "the sky is the limit."

Remember, also, that MLM is life. It is people, and as such, is an applied course in communication. And the associated motivational and awards meetings provide the opportunity to develop public speaking skills. Think about it, and you will find that whatever your survival needs, MLM can close the gap more quickly than most vehicles.

II. ESTHETIC NEEDS (DESIRES): Financial independence allows one to devote more time to the fulfillment of these needs. In this category we find:

1. **THE DESIRE FOR PERSONAL DEVELOPMENT:** Basic to life itself, is the trend toward enlightenment. Our very being cries out for progress and improvement.

2. **THE DESIRE TO HAVE FRIENDS:** Another one of our basic needs, in this area, is to be admired, to interact with others, and develop empowering relationships.

3. **THE DESIRE TO BE FREE:** Who wouldn't want the freedom to create his own lifestyle? The more we operate within our own time clock and schedule, the easier it is to experience "peace of mind."

4. **THE DESIRE TO EXPERIENCE THE FINER THINGS IN LIFE:** To be able to travel and experience the best in life is a luxury we all deserve. Why not have very simple tastes like, "The best in life will always do."

Multi-level marketing, as the "accelerated game of life," serves this group of needs even more efficiently than the first. This is true because they can be fulfilled prior to, and in the process of, generating an income.

The "game of life" is people and MLM is a people business. If you want to meet people and make new friends, MLM is it! It's possible to make more friends in a year of MLM than you have made during your entire life. MLM is an applied course in relationships, communication, and leadership.

III. CONTRIBUTION NEEDS: Here again we could list many specifics, but the "bottom line" is the need to help others, to lead them forward, to make a positive difference in their lives. The "bottom line" is we all need to make our mark in life. We do that by making a difference, and we make a difference by operating within the framework of contribution.

SURVIVAL versus CONTRIBUTION

Based upon the previous information concerning the human hierarchy of needs, we can now close the gap between failure and success in the "game of life," as well as in the "accelerated game of life." The same human phenomenon which makes life work, causes multi-level marketing to work. And it is nothing more than the flip of a mental switch, nothing more than coming from contribution rather than survival. But don't take it lightly! The increased power is like getting out of your family car into a bulldozer. Your life switches immediately from not working, to working. The attitudes of the people you meet switch immediately from rejection to acceptance, from distrust to trust. The simplicity and power of the switch is alluded to by saying, "If you want to be a loner, be interesting. If you want to be popular, be interested in others."

For as long as we come from survival, we will be trapped there. And, for us, relationships won't work, life won't work, and MLM won't work. Time after time, I have observed variations of the following MLM scenario:

John, a MLM distributor, who is fully aware of the more noble aspects of his business, presents the opportunity to his friend, Ralph. Instead of John operating within the framework of contribution, he "sells the sizzle." He tells Ralph how MLM allows him to be BOSS, to EARN WHILE HE LEARNS, to DEVELOP COMMUNICATIVE SKILLS and to BECOME FINANCIALLY INDEPENDENT. And, furthermore, John tells Ralph about the huge incomes of key distributors.

Even though all of the above are true, you may have noticed that they came directly from our list of SURVIVAL NEEDS. John's presentation is based upon his upline's approach, and, besides, it's what the average person wants to hear. John conveniently forgot to tell Ralph about the commitment, the long hours, and the price paid by those earning the big incomes. So what? That wasn't what Ralph wanted to hear anyway.

Ralph heard what he wanted too! He's been trapped in survival and, perhaps John, a friend, has found it...the way out. For the moment, John's story is a light in the darkness. Those dreams Ralph used to have begin to swell up within. Sure Ralph used to dream. He used to think his life made a difference. It's just that somewhere he lost hope. For some time now, Ralph has forced himself not to dream. "What's the use?" he would say to himself.

Poor Ralph! He's been sold by a friend for "thirty pieces of silver." Poor John! His heart was right, but society has flipped his mental switch from contribution to survival. He was just operating like most everyone else. John sold Ralph the "sizzle," rekindled his fires of hope, and, at the same time, set him up for discouragement, guilt, rejection and failure. This time, Ralph's fire may go out!

John was irresponsible. Ralph never knew what he was up against. Not only did Ralph not know the rules of the game, not have a game plan and a winning attitude, he didn't even know he was recruited into "the accelerated game of life." All he knew was, "it's a ground floor opportunity and those who get in now are going to get rich."

So Ralph's ablaze! How long is it going to last? He charges forward to sponsor a friend with the conscious thought of sharing a good deal, while subconsciously he knows he's coming from survival, greed, and the need to put food on the table. Down deep he feels like he's selling his friend for "thirty pieces of silver." He's waving a red flag that says, "Reject me." If he's not rejected, he may plunge a little deeper, but the guilt is building. After a few rejections, and an overdose of guilt, he feels like a con artist and a failure. And John wonders why Ralph avoids him, why he won't, at least, "use the products?"

The answer is simple. Ralph won't use the products because they remind him of his fiasco.

Ralph's story is so typical. It's sad and senseless. Operating within the frame of mind that is contribution creates entirely different results. Let's rewind, flip the switch, and play this story back within the framework of contribution and responsibility.

WINNING THE GREATEST GAME OF ALL

This time John has read WINNING THE GREATEST GAME OF ALL and has an entirely different image of MLM, as well as, a sense of responsibility when it comes to sponsoring.

John tells Ralph that he has chosen, as a hobby, personal development. In order to keep it exciting and challenging, he and a group of friends play a game called, "Let's Make the Most Out of Life." As a group they support and coach each other. Their purpose is "to support each other in developing the attitudes and habits that cause life to work and be fulfilling."

John gives Ralph a copy of WINNING THE GREATEST GAME OF ALL so he will have a realistic and healthy image of MLM. Their relationship starts out within a framework of straight-talk, realism and integrity. It starts off empowering, and at least has a chance.

If Ralph decides to abandon the path of least resistance and play the accelerated game, he will feel good about

himself, MLM, his products, and his opportunity to grow and be an example for others. No more guilt! Ralph is ablaze, and this time he probably won't go out. He looks forward to sharing his time and life with others. His self-respect grows every time he presents his ideas and opportunities. He is never personally rejected. How could anyone reject an offer of contribution? Sure, some of Ralph's prospects reject the opportunity to accelerate their lives. For some people, it's too confronting; for others, the timing isn't right; and others are afraid to be that "alive." The important thing is that Ralph's self-image remains healthy, and he doesn't take a rejection personally.

What a difference! All of a sudden we're going with the flow, no longer swimming upstream. The direction from which most people try to meet their needs usually ends up in a "vicious survival circle."

Thank goodness things aren't always as they seem!

What works is to ride a horse in the direction he's going. In other words, when we come from contribution, our survival and esthetic needs take care of themselves. This is especially true in multi-level marketing. Here we end up in a "precious circle" of giving and receiving.

The universal law of multi-level marketing is:

YOU GET WHAT YOU GIVE!

And, of course, we all know that we get out of life exactly what we put into it. We just need to quit forgetting it! And here we have the absolute, life-transforming value of MLM. An organization built around contribution is a constant reminder of what works in life. It is a positive, creative, empowering structure within which to operate, a structure which brings us forth out of our vicious circle.

Have you ever noticed how well life works? The only time it doesn't is when we invalidate it, when we come from "life doesn't work," when we try to duplicate the "crowd mentality." History and economics have always proven the masses to be wrong. In the stock and commodity markets the crowds always buy at the top and sell at the bottom. If you don't want your life to work, then follow the crowd; take the path of least resistance. On the other hand, if you want life to pay off on your terms, play full-out - play "the accelerated game of life." Dare to be different, dare to be a winner!

POINTS TO REMEMBER:

The coaching of this first chapter should lead us to breakthroughs in three key areas. The first area has to do with the image of multi-level marketing. Starting with you, the new image should be that of professionalism and service. Those of us willing to play the more difficult and equally rewarding "accelerated game of life" will command respect and be known as pacesetters. Starting with you, MLM is an entirely new game.

The second area deals with your own attitude and self-image. Create for yourself the attitude that life and MLM are games and hobbies to enjoy for many years to come. Use your life and MLM as vehicles through which to contribute to others. Realize that you are complete now, that you have everything necessary to lead a productive, fulfilling life. When you participate in MLM with the noble purpose of contributing to others, you automatically experience breakthroughs in your self-confidence and self-image, and you truly make a difference.

The third area of breakthrough is that of results. By being coachable and coming from contribution, your results (survival needs) take care of themselves. Think of your MLM products and income opportunity as the pleasant side-effects of your hobby. And be assured, if you and your downline have positive, healthy images of MLM and yourselves, products will be consumed and bonuses will be earned. Respect for yourself, your MLM opportunity, and your downline, coupled with the consistent application of energy, will produce the desired results. Always remember, "You get what you give."

The rest of this book will be dedicated to the specifics of MLM. You're not really in the game until you understand the rules. And Chapter Two outlines these rules. Later chapters will coach you in developing a winning strategy that's just right for you.

- **THE NEW MLM IMAGE: MLM is a New Game.**

- **YOUR NEW IMAGE: YOU Are Complete Now.**

- **BE COACHABLE**
- **COME FROM CONTRIBUTION**
- **"YOU GET WHAT YOU GIVE"**

RULES OF
THE GAME

There are rules, regulations, laws and principles which
govern all aspects of life. From time to time we have all
had collisions with the ruthless rules of reality. And it is
my contention that many people fail in life, and accelerated life (MLM), because they do not fully understand
the principles involved.

Past experience with multi-level marketing has uncovered the following seven rules, which we will refer to as principles:

1. **THE EMOTIONAL GIANT PRINCIPLE**
2. **THE INVESTMENT PRINCIPLE**
3. **THE DUPLICATION PRINCIPLE**
4. **THE PRODUCT MOVEMENT PRINCIPLE**
5. **THE WIDTH versus DEPTH PRINCIPLE**
6. **THE CONTRIBUTION PRINCIPLE**
7. **THE PERSONAL GROWTH PRINCIPLE**

THE EMOTIONAL GIANT PRINCIPLE

The Emotional Giant Principle says, "Whatever image a distributor has of himself and multi-level marketing will filter down through his organization." It seems almost mystical, and perhaps it is telepathic, but whatever it is, it works! If you are an emotional giant, distributors in your MLM family will also tend to be.

An emotional giant is a person who comes from contribution, has a healthy self-image, and looks for the good in people and circumstances. He has so much purpose and direction, so much to do, that he doesn't have much time to moan, groan and complain. And when he does, it certainly isn't in the presence of his downline. He sets an example, he sets the pace.

On the other hand, emotional midgets are those small-minded people who continually talk about other people and problems. The emotional giant talks about ideas and solutions. He is confident and unconcerned about what others think of him. His thought is "What you think about me is none of my business."

What we're talking about here is not positive thinking. I don't like positive thinking and I dislike negative thinking even more. An emotional giant's thinking is straight thinking - honest thinking - thinking which makes a difference.

The reason this principle is so critical is because we become like the people we associate with. If you want your associates to be high-performers, then you must be a high-performer. And if you want to be a high-performer, then associate with those who are. Some of the greatest opportunities for growth and motivation are the meetings and reunions associated with multi-level marketing. These social gatherings allow us to associate with others who are like-minded, and the support can be very beneficial.

Personally, I have found that the greatest factor leading to being an emotional giant is action. Many of our teammates spend so much time planning and making preparations to do something that they get very little done. We must learn to "forward the action"...to lay it on the line...to take the risk. As long as we remain immobilized by fear, we have no choice, no chance.

Several years ago I read a book titled, LIFE AFTER DEATH. It described the experiences and resulting attitudes of people who had been clinically dead and brought back to life. For most of them, life took on a whole new meaning. Rather than living in a past that no longer existed, or in a future which would never exist, they began to live in the present, moment by moment. The near-death experience shocked them into becoming emotional giants.

Wouldn't it be great if we could all have a near-death experience? Wouldn't it be great if we could attend a "near-death workshop," resulting in a renewed zest for living. Michael Cross wrote a song that went something like this: "If a doctor told you you were going to die, wouldn't you do as you please? Listen to me brother, life is just another terminal disease!"

Life is short! Decide today to become an emotional giant. Why not think of your life as one of the world's greatest corporations? Such an enterprise deserves a professional at its helm, and you will be such a professional if you think and say you are. Henry Ford once said, "If you think you can or you think you can't, you're right."

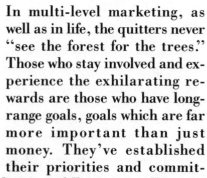

In multi-level marketing, as well as in life, the quitters never "see the forest for the trees." Those who stay involved and experience the exhilarating rewards are those who have long-range goals, goals which are far more important than just money. They've established their priorities and commitments, and the financial success follows naturally.

Life is not a "get-rich-quick" scheme, and neither is MLM. The riches of life and MLM do come, slowly but surely. The rewards, the fulfillment, is guaranteed to anyone who plays by the rules and plays full-out. And that's where our second rule comes into play.

THE INVESTMENT PRINCIPLE

The Investment Principle says, "In the beginning you do more than what you get paid for, but in the end, you get paid for more than you do." Here we find another one of life's principles which MLM accentuates. In multi-level marketing it takes from several weeks to several months to personally sponsor three key players first-level, and to help each of them sponsor players two or three levels in depth.

As more and more players join the team, the friendships and opportunities to contribute begin to multiply. It takes hard work and dedication to build the foundation of your MLM family. In the beginning your rewards and sense of fulfillment may seem small compared to your efforts. Even so, if the foundation is solid, the organization will reach a point where it will expand much more quickly than it could through your efforts alone. Once again, the financial rewards are a natural by-product. At a certain point the organization consumes and markets enough products to generate a healthy bonus check. A stable organization of dedicated players will continue to generate a similar bonus, month after month. And it's at this point you begin to get paid for more than what you do.

So the investment principle says, "Be in life and MLM for the long haul." Life is an ongoing experience and so is multi-level marketing. Set long-range plans like "retirement in 3 to 5 years." Yes, multi-level marketing can accelerate you into a comfortable retirement in 3 to 5 years, if you are a dedicated player and come from contribution. Remember, we get out of life and MLM exactly what we give!

If you don't take on this great hobby, this great opportunity to contribute, this great financial opportunity, where will you be emotionally and financially 5 years from now? Make up your mind now to invest in yourself, to invest in others, to take this path of responsibility, this path which tends to mold and shape someone just like you into a leader, a contributor. Accept the responsibility for life and the difference it can make. Be all that you can be, and lead the way for all of those who are fortunate enough to cross your path. Life and MLM allow us to duplicate our magnificence through example, and that is the subject of our third rule.

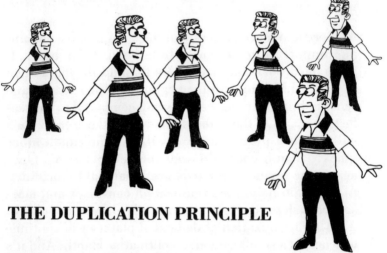

THE DUPLICATION PRINCIPLE

The Duplication Principle says, "Keep it simple." No matter how effective and successful you are in life and MLM, you'll contribute the most by being duplicatable. And the more complicated you and your techniques are, the harder it will be to duplicate you.

You may sponsor Jeanette and contribute greatly to her, but if she can't duplicate the same for Peggy, the process stops. For an organization to continue to grow in depth, the recruiting, training, and motivation must be simple and duplicatable.

Since there is no limit to how many times you can duplicate yourself, "the sky's the limit." Your downline can continue to grow and your bonus checks can continue to increase. They depend only on how well you and your downline duplicate yourselves.

And what is the most duplicatable? What is the simplest? Of course, the answer is obvious. All of us can duplicate honesty, sincerity and integrity. If we "talk straight," tell it like it is, and avoid the tendency to exaggerate and "sell the sizzle," then we will be easily and naturally duplicated.

As Don Failla points out in his book, HOW TO BUILD A LARGE SUCCESSFUL MULTI-LEVEL MARKETING ORGANIZATION, "we are never duplicated in a leg of our MLM business, until that leg is at least 3 generations deep." In other words, the duplication principle functions in a cycle of three. The cycle goes something like this: You sponsor Tom and teach him how to teach Carol to sponsor Betty. At this point, you are three generations deep, and can go away to work with another group. This leg will continue to grow. Don emphasizes, "YOU HAVE TO GO THREE DEEP! You have nothing until you are three deep and only then are you duplicated." He goes on to say that this principle is an important key for success as a MLM distributor.

YOU

TEACH
TOM

HOW TO TEACH
CAROL

TO SPONSOR
BETTY

THE PRODUCT MOVEMENT PRINCIPLE

The Product Movement Principle says, "You have to be your own best customer." As pointed out in the Emotional Giant Principle, in MLM your attitude and actions filter down through your organization. Consequently, it is imperative that you set the example of what you want duplicated downline. If you don't like and don't use your MLM products, neither will your downline!

If you are excited about the products, and find new, creative ways to use them, so will your downline! The bottom line is this: if you're not going to substitute your MLM products into your daily life wherever possible, you might as well forget building an organization. You will be wasting your time as well as the time of those you sponsor. After all, bonuses are only paid on the products which move through your MLM family. In other words, bonuses are in direct proportion to product volume, and it doesn't matter whether the products are consumed within the organization or marketed outside of it.

Products are moved in MLM much differently than they are in direct sales. In MLM you don't have to be concerned with to whom you're going to sell your products. Retail sales will occur in the process of seeking out new players. Direct selling, on the other hand, demands continual retail sales, and only 3% to 5% of our population have personalities which are compatible with such difficult selling. Research has proven that certain people are born salesmen and that sales training has little to do with their success. In direct sales, 20% of the staff move 80% of the products, or, a few salesmen move a lot of products. In MLM the opposite is true! In multi-level marketing, you have a lot of distributors, each moving only a small amount of product.

If you are going to play MLM, play full-out. Playing full-out means setting the pace and using your MLM products religiously.

THE WIDTH versus DEPTH PRINCIPLE

The Width versus Depth Principle says, "A multi-level marketing organization must have both width and depth. One without the other is unproductive."

By width, we mean the number of distributors which you personally sponsor. If you sponsor 2 people, your organization is 2-wide; if you sponsor 5, you're 5-wide, and so on. The depth of your organization comes from distributors being sponsored under your first-level. If there are distributors in the 2nd, 3rd, 4th, and 5th levels, your organization is 5-deep, and so on.

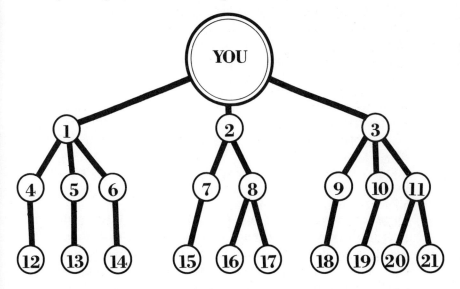

3-WIDE X 3-DEEP

Of course, you must have some width (be at least 1-wide) before you can create any depth. But the mistake most players make is to think that they need lots of width. True, the more people you sponsor, the more legs you have working. Maybe!

When you sponsor a first level distributor, it's like starting a new business. Like any other new business, it will require management and supervision. Without the personal attention needed to get the business established, it will probably go bankrupt. The person who spends most of his time starting businesses (sponsoring), and very little time supervising them, will find that those previously started will go bankrupt as quickly as new ones can be added. Before long the sponsor will be confronted with the fact that he has wasted a lot of time and energy.

So the key to this principle is to sponsor no more first-level distributors than you can properly manage. Our recommendation is to sponsor no more than 3 key players at a time. (Here again we operate within a cycle of three.) By key players, we mean those who understand the game and are willing to play full-out.

Upon sponsoring three key distributors, you and they begin to sponsor depth. Only through depth can a particular leg of your business become stable. Usually by at least the fifth generation, a high-performance player will enter the game. Chances are, he will perpetuate that leg and cause it to become a stable business. It is rare for a leg that is 8 to 10 generations deep to go bankrupt.

Organizational depth not only creates stability, but profitability as well. Even if you were 50-wide, without depth, your downline would not be large enough to generate much volume. If each of the fifty were using $40 worth of products each month, your downline volume would be $2,000. On the other hand, since your organization expands geometrically with depth, if you were only 3-wide, and each downline distributor, through 6 levels, were 3-wide, your downline would contain 1,092 distributors. 1,092 x $40 equals a volume of $43,680 per month. The bottom line is this, a downline consisting of 1,092 players is much more stable and profitable than one consisting of 50 players. Besides, think of how many more opportunities there will be to contribute within the larger organization.

Once you have coached your 3 key distributors into stable depth, and have taught them how to coach, you are ready to start another cycle of three...3-wide by at least 3-deep.

Now that you understand why "shallow width" is unstable and unprofitable, let's not underestimate the importance of "deep width." As important as depth is, it alone is not the answer. You must have both width and depth because all MLM bonus plans provide compensation to a particular downline depth. If your organization continues to grow below that level, it adds to your stability, but not necessarily to your profitability. Moreover, most MLM bonus plans require a certain amount of width to tap a certain depth. Consequently, a "one leg" MLM organization rarely generates a significant income. In other words, you can't merely sponsor one go-getter and strike it rich. The superstars are great, but MLM requires teamwork. The superstars wouldn't even have a game to play, if it were not for the rest of us. Besides, more often than not, the superstars are short-lived sparks rather than a steady glow. And there is virtue in taking the time to do it right, especially in MLM.

Ultimately, in MLM the large incomes are the result of width - stable, deep width. The reason for this can be made clear by Ronald McDonald. For example, let's say that McDonald's restaurants generate a monthly income of $5,000 each. You could own one McDonald's and earn $5,000 per month, or own five and earn $25,000. Starting all five at once might be overwhelming and lead to bankruptcy. Why not be slow but sure? Why not start one, get it running smoothly, then start another, and another, and so forth.

Multi-level marketing is a business. It is a business without many of the negative aspects of other businesses. It is a business with unlimited potential. Why not recognize it as such? Why not respect it as such? Why not treat it as such? Only those who do will benefit as such!

In summary, this principle requires one to sponsor a few key players and turn them into stable groups before sponsoring others. Sponsor, then teach...Sponsor, then teach...Sponsor, then teach!

THE CONTRIBUTION PRINCIPLE

The Contribution Principle says, "In life and MLM, we get what we give." And that is why some people get so much out of life and multi-level marketing. They merely take advantage of the unlimited opportunities to contribute to others.

We could subtitle this principle, "Sharing and Caring." And who doesn't want to be shared with and cared for? Again, we're talking about basics. The fact is others want you to share your life with them, they want you to care for them.

The phrase, "living is giving," comes to mind, as well as the story of the two seas near Galilee. The Sea of Galilee is fed by rivers and streams. It receives their contribution and passes it on. It receives, it gives, it lives. The Sea of Galilee is a living sea. On the other hand, the Dead Sea is fed by rivers and streams, but rather than passing the water on, it keeps it only to become stagnant and dead. The Dead Sea does not give; it does not live.

So go our lives. If we give, we live. And the more we give, the more we get. We have all heard that the one who teaches is the one who learns the most. Another way to put it is: "When you make a difference in another person's life, an even greater difference is made in your own."

Remember how multi-level marketing accelerates life? MLM increases our opportunities to give and, therefore, to receive. In the first chapter, we learned how to flip the switch and come from contribution rather than survival. Most people come from: "When I get, I'll give...when I get what I want, I'll be able to give to others." What doesn't work is: "Receive, then give." What does work is: "Give, then receive...Give, then receive...Give, then receive!" - the "precious circle."

THE PERSONAL GROWTH PRINCIPLE

The Personal Growth Principle says, "Multi-level marketing is a high-performance vehicle through which to experience personal growth."

NEED I SAY MORE? I could be redundant, but books that are redundant drive me up the wall. Sometimes redundance is necessary, but, more often than not, it is a waste of time and energy.

What I do want to repeat is: "Multi-level marketing can get you to wherever you want to go, faster!" Perhaps you want:

- more friends
- more opportunities to contribute
- to improve your half of relationships
- to develop your communicative skills
- to develop your leadership (coaching) skills
- to own and operate your own business
- to supplement your income

- to be the best you can be
- to become financially independent
- to play life full-out.

MLM can assist you in becoming, doing, and having, just about anything in life. Why? Because MLM is LIFE...THE ACCELERATED GAME OF LIFE.

It's rather obvious that the Accelerated Game of Life will also accentuate fear, frustration, failure, etc. It doesn't miss a trick; it's all there - life, in general. The "school of hard knocks" or the "University of Life" can now be referred to as the Multi-level Marketing University, or MLMU. I truly believe that a person playing the MLM game full-out can experience a "normal lifetime" within only a few years. MLM definitely speeds up the process, the process of life itself.

Now that you understand seven basic rules of the game, wouldn't it be great to know what stages you will go through as your play progresses? Sure, it would; and it's only fair that you do. Therefore, let's forward the action to Chapter Three, "A Player's Natural Progression."

POINTS TO REMEMBER:

THE EMOTIONAL GIANT PRINCIPLE: You become like those with whom you associate. "What you think of me is none of my business."

THE INVESTMENT PRINCIPLE: In the end, you get paid for more than what you do!

THE DUPLICATION PRINCIPLE:
Keep it simple. TEACH TOM ... HOW TO TEACH CAROL ... TO SPONSOR BETTY. "THE SKY IS THE LIMIT!" Don't sell the sizzle - talk straight.

THE PRODUCT MOVE-MENT PRINCIPLE:
"You have to be your own best customer."

THE WIDTH versus DEPTH PRINCIPLE:

DEEP WIDTH = STABLE INCOME

SHALLOW WIDTH = BANKRUPTCY!

THE PRECIOUS CIRCLE!

GIVE RECEIVE RECEIVE GIVE

THE CONTRIBUTION PRINCIPLE:
We get what we give!

**THE PERSONAL
GROWTH PRINCIPLE:**
MLM stimulates per-
sonal development.

A PLAYER'S
NATURAL PROGRESSION

Life is a continual progression, but it does so in cycles...highs and lows...ups and downs. They say that the only thing in life which is constant is change! This being true, "All things must pass." In other words, if you are currently experiencing your lowest or highest point in life, it is only a passing phenomena.

The redeeming factor, about the cycle known as you, is that it is an upward trending cycle. Not only do the highs get higher, but the lows get higher as well.

Our lives naturally progress toward enlightenment, fulfillment and satisfaction. What's natural is for our lives to work. And sometimes, when they don't appear to be working, it's only because we're trying to force things to happen, trying to play hardball with softball rules.

Life and MLM flow in a natural progression, and what works for us, as players, is to go with the flow. Another colloquial way to put it is: "We have to walk before we can run."

The whole point of this chapter is to identify the stages through which people, projects and organizations progress. Our awareness of these stages will subdue our tendency "to get the cart before the horse." We will be able to proceed one step at a time, lay a solid foundation, and not be easily discouraged. Many times we become discouraged when we're only on page 30 while wanting to be on page 50, and not knowing that page 30 is exactly where we should be.

The following list shows the natural stages of progression and how they relate to a lifetime, an athletic career and a multi-level marketing career. The associated ages and time periods are only approximations.

Stage	Lifetime	Athlete	MLM
Formulative	0-6 yrs.	Little League	1-4 weeks
Concentration	6-20 yrs.	School League	1-2 years
Momentum	20-50 yrs.	Minor League	3-5 years
Stability	50-? yrs.	Major League	Financial Independence

In keeping with our sports theme, we might say that to score you have to touch all of the bases. In other words, we can't get to stability without completing the three prior stages. Let's take them one at a time and see how they relate more specifically to multi-level marketing.

THE FORMULATIVE STAGE

In MLM, the formulative stage is that period of time when you are reading this book, especially the next chapter, "Establishing a Game Plan." This stage is the blueprint from which the MLM organization is built, the structure within which to operate. It's similar to the formulative stage of a child, where the mind patterns created dramatically affect his entire life.

Get the picture? The formulative stage is the shortest period, yet it's the most critical since it lays the track on which to run. Therefore, Chapter Four will coach you in formulating the attitudes, habits, actions, purposes, and plans which work in multi-level marketing.

THE CONCENTRATION STAGE

In MLM, the concentration stage is where we get the ball rolling. It's the time to "make hay while the sun shines." And as my mother used to say, "Anything, worth doing, is worth doing right. And doing it right usually takes time."

The time, during this stage, can range anywhere from six months of concentrated effort to several years at a more leisurely pace. The important thing to realize is that the foundation is built during this stage. The future quality and integrity of the MLM organization is set up during this period.

Some of you may want to exert an intense effort for a shorter time; but, for most, this takes the fun out of it. It becomes more like work than a hobby, and the tendency is to "burn oneself out." Remember, the more realistic and long-term approach is that of a hobby. You don't have to create a large, profitable organization overnight. Yet, don't use that thought as an "excuse" for not playing full-out. The point is to establish a comfortable, long-distance pace. The successful approach to life and MLM is that of a marathon runner, rather than that of a sprinter.

The concentration stage is where we start sponsoring width and depth, creating the organizational foundation from which the momentum stage can begin. The time involved, during the concentration phase, varies with the quality of leadership and the commitment of the players. An organization, built around strong leadership which is duplicated downline, and which contains a high percentage of serious players, will find itself in momentum long before an organization lacking these attributes.

62

THE MOMENTUM STAGE

If the formulative stage is the "blueprint" from which the "foundation" is started during the concentration stage, the momentum stage is where the "shell of the building" begins to quickly take shape. All of a sudden you begin to see results. All of a sudden the structure becomes visible.

Prior to momentum, we experience "doing more than what we get paid for." There seem to be very little visible results. Once the momentum stage gets underway, we begin to experience that part of the investment principle which is "getting paid for more than what we do." Finally, we begin to see tangible results.

In other words, once a properly built organization reaches a certain size, it seems to explode. The organization flows from concentration to momentum automatically. If you are consistently building a solid, duplicatable foundation which is based upon straight-talk and integrity, at some point you will recognize momentum. Perhaps you suddenly realize that your organization is growing by leaps and bounds, and that the growth seems to be effortless. That's momentum. It's exciting; but, like everything else, it is not permanent. The longer you operate within the concentration stage, the longer the momentum stage will last. Consequently, the momentum stage can be extended by extending your period of concentrated effort. And, furthermore, momentum can be renewed by another period of concentrated effort.

By spending one to two years in the concentration phase, your momentum should last another one to three years.

Even during the momentum stage, you need to "ongoingly" provide coaching and set an example for your organization. Momentum is exhilarating. Flow with it and enjoy every moment.

THE STABILITY STAGE

In our example, the stability stage is where the purpose is fulfilled for designing and constructing the building. At this point, the tenants move in, utilize, and maintain the structure. Regarding our MLM organization, the stability stage involves gradual improvements, not just maintenance. Here we experience a gradual growth and expansion of the MLM organization. Remember, life's natural tendency is improvement, expansion. In other words, mere maintenance in life or MLM is unstable. This stage is graphically represented below by a line which is trending upward. In other words, a flat line (maintenance) or a downward trending line (contraction) is not stable in life or multi-level marketing.

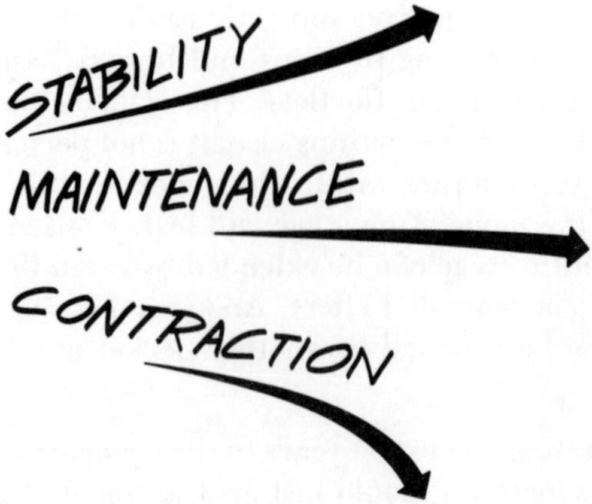

STABILITY

MAINTENANCE

CONTRACTION

The following graph illustrates the natural progression through all four stages.

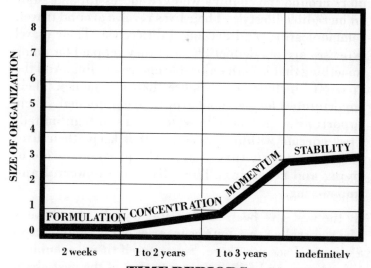

For the person who has built their organization around contribution, the stability stage can provide a financial freedom and lifestyle second to none. This organization provides a stable income which is gradually increasing. The beauty of it all, and the reason it provides you freedom, is because the income is totally independent of risk capital, overhead, employees, inventories, complicated accounting, working for someone else, a rigid work schedule (8 to 5), etc.

To a certain degree, the stability stage provides an income which is independent of you. You may travel around the world with your family and return to find that your organization and income are larger. But that's not to say that during the stability stage you can become less responsible. Your organization may require less time and be less demanding, but the need for your leadership and coaching will continue.

The stability stage is truly the "big carrot" in multi-level marketing. We have all heard about those distributors around the country who are successful and enjoy an incredible lifestyle. Their lives revolve around travel, communicating, and making a difference. Their travel expenses are tax deductible, and they get paid for doing something that is both enjoyable and rewarding. And the "pay off" includes much more than just money. Their opportunities for personal growth are unlimited. Their opportunities to contribute to others are unlimited. They operate within a structure that keeps their lives on track, a structure that is the precious circle of giving and receiving. Their lives are powerful and empowering.

By the way, I've been talking about you! (The above is who you really are.) Your heart cries out to contribute in a big way. I see you there. See yourself there, commit to being there, and follow the game plan of the next chapter. The game plan is like a roadway to, into and through each stage of the process.

POINTS TO REMEMBER:

Our lives naturally progress toward enlightenment.

THE FORMULATIVE STAGE:
Designing your MLM future.

THE CONCENTRATION STAGE:
Building your MLM foundation.

THE MOMENTUM STAGE:
Your MLM organization becomes
visible.

THE STABILITY STAGE:
The big carrot in MLM.

ESTABLISHING A GAME PLAN

Through Chapter One, we became aware of how multi-level marketing is a vehicle through which we can make our mark in life. Furthermore, we developed healthy images of ourselves, MLM and the resulting relationship. In Chapter Two we took a look at the rules of the accelerated game and found that the key rule is contribution. Contribution makes the world of MLM "go around."

Progressing to Chapter Three, we got a "bird's eye view" of the building process and the approximate length of time associated with each stage. Now, in Chapter Four, we are going to proceed through each stage step-by-step. We could refer to this chapter as the "nuts and bolts" of MLM. It is the 4th corner of our structure.

THE FORMULATIVE STAGE

As you recall from the last chapter, the formulative stage is the design, the ultimate integrity, the bottom line of our structure. In your MLM career, this is the stage where your blueprint is created. Everything in the physical universe began as an idea or thought. Your MLM organization will be just as strong, or just as weak, as you design it to be.

By taking the small amount of time required to design your MLM future, and, by putting it down in black and white, you will automatically be a quantum leap ahead of the crowd. Who would consider trying to build a large, multi-faceted, high-rise office complex without a blueprint? The answer, of course, is no one! By the same token, who would consider building a large, multi-faceted, complex MLM organization without a blueprint? Oddly enough, the answer is: almost everyone!

Can you believe it? Why would anyone even try to build something without the foggiest idea of what it is supposed to look like? The fact is that most people approach not only MLM this way, but their entire lives.

Absolutely essential for you to get from where you are now to where you want to be, is to know where you want to be. Once you've decided where, you must know how to get there. Since the "how" probably involves knowledge, method, time, effort and expense, you must be willing to do whatever it takes to get there. I'm talking about a commitment...a no alternative, "burn your bridges behind you" commitment. The rest is history. You will get there. The universe works that way. Personally, I believe that the universe was set up to honor any and all clearly defined intentions backed by absolute commitment.

Now is the time to take a stand to be different. You can't afford to follow the crowd! The price is your life! Throughout history the masses have collected evidence that life doesn't work, that it is effect rather than cause. Why even consider the crowd's evidence? They never intended for life to work in the first place. Let me put it this way: What society's evidence has gotten you is 30,000 intercontinental ballistic missiles (ICBM's) pointed at your head.

Now is the time to take a stand on the evidence collected by those whose lives work. From this moment forward, let's collect evidence to support that:

- you are whole, capable, adequate and complete.
- you make a living doing what you love to do.
- your income always exceeds your expenses.
- the less you work the more money you make.
- you deserve and can afford the best in life.
- your commitment is health, wealth and sufficiency.

Those people whose lives work this way are no different from you or me. The difference, in results, has to do with intention and commitment. To produce outstanding results with your life, you may only need to design a specific, written plan and make a no- alternative, "burn-your-bridges-behind-you" commitment. It works in life. It works in MLM. And besides, if you're not playing fully committed, you have no chance to win - zero! What you are learning and getting ready to apply to multi-level marketing can be applied to all aspects of life.

So, here in the formulative stage, you are going to decide where you want to be. You are going to create a track which will carry you to your 6-month, 1-year, 3-year, 6-year, and 10-year destinations. Without a track to run on and a destination to move toward, your life will be spent on detours to nowhere.

First of all, you need to decide upon your final destination and the stopovers along the way. Then, the track will be created to keep your path as direct as possible. The destinations are your desires, and the track is your commitment to contribute. In other words, the most direct path to what you want is to contribute to others.

The following blueprint includes the things which you want to be, do, have and contribute. Each category has one or more examples.

Turn the page and start creating your own blueprint.

SIX MONTHS FROM NOW:

What I want to be:

I am an Emotional Giant.
I am committed to health and wealth.
I am an example for my downline.

_____

_____

_____

_____

What I want to do:

I am jogging daily and maintaining my ideal
    weight.
I am developing 3 empowering relationships.
I am using my MLM products regularly and
    assisting the growth of my downline.

_____

_____

_____

_____

What I want to have:

I have more than 40 committed players on
    my team.
I have $500 worth of my MLM products in
    my possession.
I have a new, black Cadillac Cimarron coupe.

_____

_____

_____

_____

What I want to contribute:

I am coaching and supporting 3 first-level
distributors.
I am active in the school PTA.

_____

_____

_____

_____

ONE YEAR FROM NOW:
                                    DATE _____

What I want to be:

I am a confident, capable coach.
I am one who operates out of integrity.

_____

_____

_____

_____

What I want to do:

I am developing 6 empowering relationships.
My family and I are taking 2 tax-deductible, MLM
vacations per year.

_____

_____

_____

_____

What I want to have:
I have more than 80 committed players on
    my team.
I have a monthly MLM income exceeding $500.
I have a new 3,000 square-foot home in Ranch
    Acres.

_____

_____

_____

_____

What I want to contribute:
I am coaching and supporting 6 first-level
    distributors.
I am teaching my Sunday School class.

_____

_____

_____

_____

THREE YEARS FROM NOW:
DATE _____

What I want to be:
I am a confident, effective public speaker.
I am in demand because of my leadership abilities.

_____

_____

_____

_____

What I want to do:

I am maintaining at least 15 empowering
relationships.
I am traveling and motivating others regularly.

_____

_____

_____

_____

What I want to have:

I have more than 500 committed players on
my team.
I have a monthly MLM income exceeding $3,000
per month.
My net worth exceeds $200,000.

_____

_____

_____

_____

What I want to contribute:

I am coaching and supporting 12 first-level
distributors.
I take time to make people smile wherever I go.

_____

_____

_____

_____

SIX YEARS FROM NOW:

DATE _____

What I want to be:

I am a powerful person who contributes to
whomever I meet.
I am committed to being the best I can be.

_____

_____

_____

_____

What I want to do:

I am maintaining at least 20 empowering
relationships.
I recreate and travel extensively.

_____

_____

_____

_____

What I want to have:

I have a large, stable MLM organization.
I have a monthly MLM income exceeding $10,000
per month.
My net worth exceeds $1,000,000.
We own a luxurious estate home.

_____

_____

_____

_____

What I want to contribute:

I am a light in the darkness, an example of health, wealth, and happiness.

_____

_____

_____

_____

TEN YEARS FROM NOW:

DATE _____

What I want to be:

I am an international person.
I am committed to making a world-wide difference with my life.

_____

_____

_____

_____

What I want to do:

I am maintaining at least 30 empowering relationships.
My family and I actively participate in snow skiing, scuba diving, sailing, flying, fishing, and sightseeing.

_____

_____

_____

_____

What I want to have:
    I am financially independent.
    I have a MLM income exceeding $50,000 per
       month.
    I have a net worth in excess of $5,000,000.

_____

_____

_____

What I want to contribute:
    I devote time each month to inspiring others.
    My life makes a real difference for others.

_____

_____

_____

The ten-year projection provides continual long-range planning, because you should update it at least every six months. As you create your personal blueprints, make sure that they are what you really want, that they include all areas of your life, that you state them positively, and that you are committed to fulfilling them. Before reading any further, go back and write at least two items in each category.

Go ahead! I'll be right here when you get back!

Okay! Now that you've made your personal requests to the Universe for what you want, let's lay the track that will take you there.

Earlier we got a glimpse of what I consider to be a universal law. And, I'll put it this way: "The way to tap into the flow of universal abundance is to come from contribution and be absolutely committed to specific, written intentions." In other words, write down a plan involving contribution and take a stand on it.

Making commitments and keeping them are essential for life to work. Without commitment, life is death. To experience "aliveness," we must commit ourselves to projects and purposes which make a contribution. But not only do we have to make commitments, we have to keep them. If you don't keep your commitments, your life will not work. If you do, it will. It's just that simple.

This chapter will be very informative, but you will probably find it very motivational as well. Talk about hope...talk about excitement...talk about taking the pressure off! If you can accept the evidence that I've collected about how simple MLM and life is, you're going to be ecstatic.

Evidence has proven to me that a life set in motion upon the right track, and kept simple, guarantees the desired results.

A few years ago, I authored a book titled, AWARENESS DYNAMICS, in which I creatively and persuasively presented a way to reprogram our mental computers, and to accomplish our goals through utilizing the powerful subjective level of the brain/mind complex, which is identifiable as alpha brainwave patterns on an electro-encephalograph. Hundreds of books have been written about positive thinking, inspiration, repetition of positive affirmations, etc. Thousands of "how to" books have told us that if we will do this ritual, or that ritual, we will succeed.

Evidence indicates that these books are too often a bunch of crap, perhaps even my own. They sell because a good idea is always more seductive than the truth. I know that you're about to drown in good ideas, and need to be rescued by the simple truth. And, by the way, I'm not trying to sell you anything. Truth is truth, whether you, or I, or anyone else believes it. The only things which we have to believe are our judgments, opinions, and prejudices (which our survival mechanism won't let go of). Probably, that little voice in the back of your head (your voice over) just said, "Could that be the truth, or is that just his opinion?" And it doesn't matter. It doesn't matter, because who we really are is not our survival system of opinions, beliefs, judgments, prejudices and the like (which for simplification, we'll label our "stuff"). Thank goodness we can transcend our "stuff," because we're never going to change it, no matter how many "how to" books we read.

Ninety percent of our "stuff" was firmly in place by age three. Our survival mechanism latched onto every ounce of "stuff" it could. The basic theme of our "stuff" is: "To survive I need to make others wrong and me right." Of course, as long as we operate from our "stuff," we'll be trapped in the survival circle, where life never works.

Oops! There it goes again…that little voice saying, "Why doesn't he get to the point." Well, here it is. The simple truth is:

> ● Life works! Being in the flow of abundance is natural. The river of abundance flows in the realm of contribution, but not in the realm of survival. To go with the flow, we merely need to flip our mental switch from survival to contribution, observe our "stuff" but not let it run us, and build a boat to ride in.

The boat is merely the track which we are going to create as we proceed. It might clarify this concept to think of this track as a structure within which to operate, a structure that keeps you within the realm of contribution. We'll design this structure in such a way that it will keep you flowing with contribution, like the walls of a "water slide" channel the water and you right to a big splash. What we want to do is create a structure or track which will automatically transport you to making a big splash in MLM and life. All you need do is "push off." Gravity will take care of the rest.

I hope that where we're headed is clear, and, in case it's not, I'll summarize:

1. Your life will work automatically, as long as you come from a commitment to contribute.

2. You can't get rid of your "stuff;" it will try to keep you in survival; your "voice over" will keep telling you that your life doesn't work. But your willingness to contribute allows you to operate outside of your "stuff." It allows you to be big enough to observe your "stuff" and tell your "voice over," "Thanks for sharing, but my life does work."

3. A precise, black and white, written statement of who you are, who you're going to be, and how you're going to get there, creates a track with guardrails which prevent derailment. Of course, your "stuff" tries to get you off track, but, as you trend that way, the guard rails slap you right in the face - a rude awakening, but exactly what you needed and wanted.

So, let's start laying your track. It will be laid in stages. As we get into the concentration phase of your MLM business, we will lay down some commitments regarding sponsoring, supporting your upline and downline, etc.

Even though we may look at it in different ways, and in more depth as we proceed, it seems appropriate to discuss another truth at this time. And this is the biggy! This is the one which will transform your life. The more you align yourself with this one, the more difference you are going to make. And here it is:

●

"The only way to stay in the realm of contribution is to sponsor others into it."

Sponsoring is the front line; it keeps you in the game. By the way, it's the only game in town. For, in all of life, people are selling or conning you, or you are sponsoring them into the realm of contribution. Everyday you let people sell you on why they should stay in their "stuff," or you sponsor them. You "sell out," or you make a difference. We cannot experience transformation in our own lives without participating in the transformation of others.

So, your stand should be to sponsor others into the realm of contribution. And a stand is like the Alamo, - this is it, to the end! The more people you sponsor, the more contribution becomes a part of you, and, not only does your capacity to contribute expand, but it becomes increasingly easier to stay on track.

By now, the big picture should be taking shape. You should be starting to comprehend the magnitude of what we're doing. We're not just sponsoring others into our MLM opportunity. We're sponsoring them into life itself. MLM is merely a *modus operandi* which allows us to make the transition from the land of the living dead (survival) to the land of aliveness (contribution).

Could we possibly have a more noble purpose for our lives? Of course not! And the "icing on the cake" is the fact that multi- level marketing allows us to not only earn a living, but to even tap into the universal flow of abundance. Wow! I've just been responsored. It's such a thrill to have been able to transcend "stuff" long enough to have recognized MLM for what it really is, to put it on paper, and to contribute it to you. I'm already experiencing an exhilaration as a result of this contribution, and no one has even read it yet. And, by the way, let's add this to our evidence that life works when we contribute.

At this point, there is very little doubt in my mind about your desire and willingness to take the first step. It's now time to "push off." It's time to "swing out." It's time to "take your stand."

STEP 1 IS MY STAND DATE _____
TIME _____

Who I am:
Example: I am a being, desiring to make my mark on life. I want nothing more than the opportunity to make a difference.

_____

_____

_____

_____

_____

_____

Who I will be:

Example: From this moment forward I commit to
play life full-out, to come from contribution.
My commitment is to a life that works so well that
all who see it are moved toward health, wealth, and
fulfillment.

_____

_____

_____

_____

_____

BOTTOM LINE: MY PURPOSE IN LIFE
IS CONTRIBUTION!

How I'm going to get there:

This part is still my responsibility and my
contribution to you. It's the track and we'll be
creating it throughout this chapter.

88

THE CONCENTRATION STAGE

During the previous formulative stage, we determined who you want to be, and where you want to be, in 6 months, 1 year, 3 years, 6 years and 10 years. The quality of what we do from this point forward will be determined by the quality you've already designed into it. And, you might note that there aren't different qualities of commitments. You either commit, or you don't. So what did you do? Bring your integrity all the way up for this, and if it's necessary, go back and rework your formative stage. Think big; create big; play big. Swing out there and be big. Step way out there and burn those bridges. After all, you're going to find your life, and you're going to win.

Go ahead, I'll still be here when you get back!

THE MLM COMPANY

There are a number of good multi-level marketing companies, but, unfortunately, there are more new and unstable ones than there are established ones. Since this book is being written for all distributors, no matter what their company affiliation, rather than recommending companies, we'll just outline what to look for.

Your success in MLM depends mainly on you, not the company. Of course, the company staying in business helps. The beauty of building your MLM organization around the principles in this book is the fact that its integrity is not dependent upon the company. If the company folds, the organization can be channeled into another company. But, let me caution you. Make sure you are in the right company to begin with. Never "switch horses in the middle of the stream."

So what do we look for in a company and in products or services to sell? Consider the following:

1. If the products or services are consumable, you will have repeat business.

2. The products or services should be high-quality and priced comparably with similar retail products or services, when the comparison is "apples to apples." (In many cases, products sold through direct selling are either highly concentrated or are superior in quality.)

3. There should be an adequate supply of the products or services.

4. The products or services should be attractively packaged, convenient and pleasant to use.

5. The company should be stable and have a long-term commitment to its future. Preferably it has made it over the "two-year business hump." Most of those who fail do so during the

first two years.

6. The company's image is critical. Quality needs to be evident in all literature, products, personnel, etc.

7. In the area of direct sales via network marketing, the ideal situation is for the company to handle the distribution of products and the calculation and disbursement of commission checks.

The above logistics being in tact, the rest is up to you. As a matter of fact, I consider the company's effect on your business to be no more than 20%. The other 80% lies totally within your control.

STEP 2 IS CHOOSING THE RIGHT MLM COMPANY

THE COMPANY'S NAME, ADDRESS AND PHONE NUMBER IS:

_____

_____

_____

I am committed to building my organization through the channel provided by this company. Mistakes will be made, but, as long as the company is committed to the "grass roots" distributors, and is doing its best, I'll be committed to it and do my best. And above all, I will always look for the good and never be disloyal, or even talk negatively about the company.

My Signature: _____

PRODUCT AND LITERATURE KNOWLEDGE

Prior to inflicting yourself upon the unsuspecting, you need to, at least, know the basics about your products and how to fill out distributor applications and product order forms. This information is simple to learn and won't take a lot of time, if you tackle it head on. Your sponsor and your company's training manual will have you knowledgeable in no time.

The best way to become excited about your products is to use them. Consequently, if at all possible, your initial product purchase should include one of each item, or, at least, a good selection of items. Take this step seriously because you can't sell from an empty wagon, and you can't talk intelligently about products you haven't personally used. Much of this initial inventory will be used for display and written off as a deductible business expense.

A true commitment to your business also includes your pocketbook. And the larger your initial investment, the easier it is to consider yourself as being in business. Your initial purchase may range anywhere from several hundred to several thousand dollars. My own initial purchase, in May of 1983, amounted to $2,492.65. With that invested, I wasn't about to "fiddle around." If your initial purchase will be substantial, take your time and get the products and literature which will move quickly through your organization as samples and downline purchases. (In addition, they will be retail items and products which you will personally consume.)

Above all, remember, that in multi-level marketing we must be our own best customer. We must set an example of personal volume for our downline - that is, in product usage and retail selling.

Besides our initial purchase, we need to commit to purchasing at least fifty dollars worth of products each and every month. Remember, the more you put into your business, the more you'll receive in return.

STEP 3 IS MY PERSONAL VOLUME COMMITMENT

At this moment, I commit to an initial product purchase amounting to $ _____. Furthermore, I commit to purchasing at least $ _____ worth of products each month, beginning _____ , 19 ____ . These products will be used for samples, retail sales, and personal consumption.

As you already know, the concentration stage is where we start producing the physical results which will start moving us toward the goals created in the formulative stage. If you are comfortable with your blueprint, your next step is to sponsor your 3 first- level key players. There are dozens of ways to introduce people to MLM, but those most widely used are:

1. one-on-one
2. home parties
3. group meetings
4. organizations
5. direct mail

Personally, I consider it impossible to meet your sponsorship responsibilities by sponsoring organizations, or by sponsoring through the mail. As a matter of fact, anyone sponsored outside of your immediate area should not be considered a key player. Remember, a key player is one with whom you can develop an empowering relationship.

I'm not saying that you shouldn't sponsor a "long distance" friend or relative. I am saying that if you do, you must, at least, see that he gets a copy of this book, that he reads it and discusses it with you. Anything short of that would be irresponsible on your part.

Experience has shown that the most duplicatable method of sponsoring is one-on-one. All of us have friends and associates with whom we can schedule a visit. This book is undoubtedly the best one-on-one recruiting tool ever available. You might get started by asking 1 to 5 of your prospects to read it, so that the two of you can discuss it in a few days. After reading it, they will either want to play or they won't. The key is presenting the book in such a way that they actually read it. You might say something like, "This book presents simple truths in such a way that lives are being transformed as a result of reading it." Every situation will be different, and you will find a way which will work for you.

For those people who won't read the book, you might want to give them a WINNING THE GREATEST GAME OF ALL cassette tape. Again, you might want to have several copies circulating at one time.

The second most effective and duplicatable way to introduce others to MLM is the home party. Home gatherings among friends are "laid back" and non-threatening. It's usually easy to get a few friends over to your house. On the other hand, it is rather difficult to get prospects to a group meeting held in a motel or office - there exists quite a resistance level because so many people have been lied to and tricked into going to an opportunity meeting. In my opinion, the large public meetings should be held no more than once a month and should be for training, inspiration, fellowship, and recognition. Of course, those persons thinking about becoming players should be invited. When organized around the above purposes, the public meetings have tremendous value.

Now, back to the home introductory party. It should be very short and very simple! If not, it will seem like work and it will not be duplicatable. Later, we'll have a complete written script for a home party, but, for now, you might consider the following outline:

1. Welcome guests and introduce speaker.
2. Discuss MLM as the "accelerated game of life" and how a long-term approach, based on the principles in WINNING THE GREATEST GAME OF ALL, virtually assures success.
3. Make certain that the guests realize that MLM is no longer what they used to know it as.
4. Demonstrate and sample some of your key products.
5. Close the meeting within a maximum time of one hour. If you ask the guests to sponsor at the meeting, make certain that they know what they are committing to.
6. It might be better to ask each guest to read this book, and to set up an appointment with him one-on-one.

Remember, above all, keep it simple. Since most MLM bonus plans are complicated, the new prospect or distributor shouldn't even be confronted with it, until he has at least read this book.

Using these simple guidelines, you should be able to sponsor your first set of 3 key players without much complication. Don't be greedy! Don't consider sponsoring more than three until all of their first-level distributors are 3-wide - that is, until you have 3, 9 and 27 distributors in your first, second and third generations, respectively.

As mentioned earlier, you may want to sponsor a friend or relative who lives outside of your area, but don't consider him as one of your key three. If you can maintain a relationship with him by phone, if he operates within our guidelines, if the products are available and he commits, he might make it. But don't depend on it.

STEP 4 IS MY SPONSORSHIP COMMITMENT

Today's date is _____ and I commit to personally sponsor 3, and only 3, first-level key distributors. To be considered key distributors, they must live within 25 miles of me; they must have read this book and made the associated commitments. I commit to having all three sponsored by

_____ (45 days maximum).

Secondly, I commit to encouraging and helping each of my key distributors to sponsor 3 key distributors. I plan to have this second generation complete with 9 distributors

by _____ (90 days maximum).

Thirdly, I commit to encouraging and helping my first-level distributors to assist their key distributors in sponsoring 3 each. In other words, I will help sponsor my 27 third-level

distributors by _____ (150 days maximum).

If any of the 39 distributors in these first three generations decide not to keep their commitments, I will replace or help replace them. Once all 39 positions are filled with key players, it will be appropriate for me to sponsor my second set of 3 first- level distributors.

THE BIMONTHLY FORUM

In multi-level marketing it is absolutely essential to be loyal and committed to your sponsor and to the people you personally sponsor. What I call the bimonthly forum meetings keep your commitment alive, and ensure the integrity of these three levels: your sponsor, you, and your first generation.

The meeting is a forum in the sense that its purpose is to be a mutually empowering discussion. The forum consists of a distributor and his key players. The forum discussion might take place in conjunction with a breakfast, luncheon, dinner, etc. Personally I prefer a dinner forum involving both spouses and taking place at each of the participants' homes on a rotating basis. Be creative and see that they make a difference. For example, if your MLM products were food, each couple could bring a covered dish consisting of a new recipe.

What it amounts to is that each distributor attends one forum every week. Every other week you attend your sponsor's forum, while having your downline forum during the alternate weeks. In other words, you might attend a forum with your sponsor and his other first-level distributors during the first and third weeks of each month, and attend a forum with your first-level distributors during the second and fourth weeks.

The forums are vital for two reasons. The first reason is based on the fact that we become like the people with whom we associate. The key players on the first levels above and below us provide vital coaching, support, and empowerment. The second reason is because the forums provide a "sure fire" way to maintain integrity throughout the organization. They are part of the structure, or track, which keeps us on course and in the game.

* We can't move ahead until the importance of this step is clear.

* The purpose of the forums is to eliminate what was previously the most serious problem in multi-level marketing - turnover. The forums help to eliminate the dropouts or "quitters."

* Prior to WINNING THE GREATEST GAME OF ALL, people were sponsored into multi-level marketing without knowing the rules of the game, without having a game plan, and without making a commitment! No wonder people quit! Our first four steps educate and train us, so that what is left is empowering each other to have integrity and to keep commitments. Can you imagine how powerful an organization would be if each distributor assumed the responsibility for his own commitment, both making and keeping it? Can you imagine how much pressure it would take off of you?

The forums serve as a weekly reminder that, if you're going to play, you're going to play by the rules. Attendance at your sponsor's forum is a statement to him (by the way, any time I use a masculine pronoun, I mean the feminine as well, that is, him or her, etc.) that you are a committed player. As long as you are attending, he knows that he does not need to replace you. And integrity demands that you let your sponsor know, if at any time, you decide not to keep your commitment. Don't just miss the forums and leave it up to him to figure it out.

So, you see, attending your sponsor's forum is vital. Unless you do, you cannot expect anyone to attend yours. So the important thing is for you to keep your commitments, and to prove it through forum participation. Your commitment and participation create space for your distributors to be committed and to participate. Your integrity will show up in your downline. Always remember that who you are and what you do will be duplicated. Not only must you be your own best customer, you must be the most committed as well.

In summary, the bimonthly forums promote integrity and identify the lack of it. No longer do we have the pressure of worrying about downline commitment. We need only keep ourselves true and empower our first generation to do likewise.

You might ask, "What if one of my three key players looses his commitment?" In that case, you merely replace him. If he has sponsored someone, you assume the sponsorship duties for this grandchild. The abandoned grandchild is invited to your forums, and this procedure would continue downline to the third generation, but not beyond. Of course, this is not a "hard and fast" rule, but, in most cases, the numbers and logistics beyond the third - level reach proportions that become overwhelming. And remember, this is to be fun, not overwhelming!

If you have 3 key players, one drops out, and you consider his distributors as though they were first-level, you
still replace the first-level dropout. Your commitment
requires that you keep at least three key distributors
first-level.

The forum is part of our track (structure). It serves to
keep the organization in commitment and to recognize
the need for repairs. What we have is:

1. Each distributor is personally responsible for his own commitment and for
   providing his sponsor with "proof positive" of such.
2. Each distributor is personally responsible to keep at least 3 committed distributors first-level.
3. Each distributor monitors his organization through three generations. He
   is ultimately responsible for 3 first-
   level, 9 second-level, and 27 third-
   level players.

And that's it! You don't need to feel responsible for a
downline of five thousand people. Just thinking about it
is overwhelming. If each of us maintain integrity
through three levels, the rest will take care of itself. If
each of us is committed to making a difference through
three generations, the entire downline will benefit.

It all sounds simple, and it is, and it isn't! Believe me,
prior to this handbook, the task was somewhat impossible. But by using WINNING THE GREATEST GAME
OF ALL as your organizational Bible, the task does become somewhat simple. And here's why, assuming all

participants have read it:

1. Everyone knows what they are up against; they know the rules of the game, and more importantly, they know what is expected of them.
2. Everyone is aware of the costs, as well as the potential rewards.
3. Everyone, at least, understands the "Contribution Principle" and what it means to make a difference.
4. Everyone knows about the different stages through which he will progress.
5. Everyone has a blueprint for success, has committed to success, and supports each other in achieving success.
6. Most important of all, everyone has a game plan, a step-by-step procedure which, when followed, produces the desired results.
7. To play, or not to play, that is the question? And whoever answers, "to play," plays by the rules. In other words, he who plays WINNING THE GREATEST GAME OF ALL, plays by the rules...full-out.
8. Whether a player's word is as good as gold, or as worthless as a tinker's damn, becomes quite apparent through the bimonthly forum. He is either in or he's out, and the "dead weight" can be quickly eliminated.

Even though all persons present at the forum participate, the sponsor is responsible for the agenda. He
picks the discussion topic and has sufficient comments
or questions to stimulate the group. Since this can be a
challenging project, and since this kind of ongoing
support is vital, we provide you with a Network Training
Program. Each month it provides you with a power-
packed forum topic. Each topic confronts the group
with yet another reason to play the "accelerated game of
life" with commitment. THE TRAINING PROGRAM
will be discussed in detail in the appendix.

STEP 5 IS MY PARTICIPATION IN THE FORUM

My signature below indicates my commitment to
participate in a forum discussion every week. I consider
these meetings to be "high priority" and will not allow
anything other than spiritual, family, and career matters
to interfere with them. I agree to host two per month, and
to attend the two hosted by my sponsor.

My Signature _____

FORUM SCHEDULE FOR REOCCURRING DAYS, TIMES AND LOCATIONS

	WEEK	DAY	TIME	LOCATION
SPONSOR'S:				
MINE:				

FORUM SCHEDULE FOR VARIABLE DAYS, TIMES AND LOCATIONS

SPONSOR'S:	MONTH	DAY	TIME	LOCATION

MINE:	MONTH	DAY	TIME	LOCATION

By continuing to go three-wide by three-deep while maintaining "our" kind of commitment and integrity, you could find your organization moving into the momentum stage in as little as 3 to 6 months - the time period being inversely proportional to your effort. One great aspect of MLM is that we get paid what we're worth, or, as previously noted, we get out of it exactly what we put into it.

THE MOMENTUM STAGE

In Chapter Three we learned that, as our concentrated effort causes our organization to move into the momentum stage, we begin to experience rapid growth, because no longer are we alone. We have duplicated ourselves, and the effects of geometric progression are becoming apparent.

 The momentum stage can be an exciting time when you seem to have the "tiger by the tail." Many people have failed in multi-level marketing because they became so infatuated with this phase that they lost sight of what produced it. Many things can happen psychologically, and most are bad.

At this point, some people become convinced that they are invincible, that their organization will expand forever, and they "bet on the come." We might refer to this trap as the "high-roller" syndrome. We could discuss it for hours, but the bottom line is: they spend money which they don't have. And if it doesn't come, or if it doesn't come soon enough, it's multi-level marketing's fault. They destroy their own image of MLM, and, the sad part is, their organization is destroyed at the same time.

I call the second trap the "lost lover" syndrome. This is the situation where the distributor falls deeply in love with the momentum stage. And, believe me, it has a way of romancing you. It's an exciting relationship, but, when the "new wears off," the distributor begins to feel neglected. His attitude can deteriorate to the point where he feels like he has been "dumped," and he will want to end the relationship, meaning his involvement, in MLM. What we must realize is that the new wears off of everything in life. We must be aware of it and be prepared for it.

Yet another syndrome is one I call "spoiled rotten." Organizational growth is so natural and easy during the momentum period. It's so easy, it can spoil you. You begin to think that momentum is the way it was meant to be. You want it that way, or not at all. The tendency is to completely lose sight of what you did to create momentum. Without an understanding of how concentration and momentum are interrelated, it's hard to figure out that to have more momentum, you just go back to basics.

We could ramble on, but by now it's clear - long term success demands that we never loose sight of our very simple steps. As soon as we do, it's all downhill.

The main point of this section is to continue:

- **to come from contribution with commitment.**
- **to be loyal to our company.**
- **using our products faithfully.**
- **sponsoring, coaching, and empowering.**

And that's it! Those are the basics that work every time. The only "missing link" is whether or not you will go through the motions. And that part is completely within your control and your responsibility.

So, to keep momentum rolling, keep in touch with the basics. Keep them alive and a part of you.

THE MONTHLY FORUM

Organizational growth during the momentum stage creates the possibility for public meetings where the expanding family of distributors can get to know each other. When the time is right, and it will be apparent, the organization can be benefited through fellowship and acknowledgement. We all desire the personal satisfaction which we receive through interacting with others and by being appreciated by others.

Most monthly forums will involve enough participants to require booking a motel meeting room. Since these types of facilities are rather expensive, it is imperative that everyone be willing to chip in. The costs can usually be covered at around five dollars per person, payable upon arrival at the door.

As you have probably already noticed, the number 3 continues to play an important role in our business. We use it again in the process of notifying the downline of special events and meetings. Rather than one person trying to inform hundreds of distributors, each distributor informs the key players in his first three levels. Each distributor has a mailing list of, at least, one set of 39 key players.

We suggest that you purchase letter size sheets of address labels and type up a master which will allow you to reproduce them on a copy machine. The next chapter, The Scoreboard, will provide you with a record-keeping system which will help you organize this area.

Now, back to the monthly forum! To be acknowledged is vital, and the primary acknowledgement should be for the keeping of commitments rather than for the advancement to bonus levels. Following is a sample of an acknowledgement session which could be led by the master of ceremonies:

1. Would everyone please stand and acknowledge each other for being here. (Applause)

2. Would those of you who are committed to making a contribution to others through our business, who are loyal to

   _____(your company), and who use our products, remain standing. Please acknowledge each other.

3. Please remain standing if you have at least 3 first-level distributors who are equally committed. (Applause)
4. Those who have at least 9 second-level committed distributors, remain standing. (Applause)
5. If you have at least 27 committed players in your third generation, please continue to stand. (Applause)
6. Keep standing if you have at least 6 first-level distributors who are committed to what we're up to. (Applause)
7. The "MC" continues in this manner until only 1 to 5 remain standing. These last few are asked to come to the front of the room, and in several minutes, tell what about their business enables them to stay committed.
8. Records should be kept so that "the leaders of the pack" are acknowledged each month, but, each meeting has new people telling their stories. In other words, those who continue to come forward each month should receive special praise, without taking any glory away from the newcomers.

ADDITIONAL NOTES

Depending on the group's willingness to devote time and money to the forum, it can range all the way from a simple, short meeting, to a covered dish dinner or banquet.

With each distributor notifying all of the players in his first three levels, there will be some overlapping. But as you know so well, it's better to be safe than sorry. The overlap will help close the gap created by anyone who might be irresponsible.

THE STABILITY STAGE

The stability stage is our ultimate MLM destination. Like momentum, it evolves naturally. As the excitement and glamour of momentum phases into stability, if we understand it and have an appropriate attitude, we can have the peace-of-mind and sense of financial security that everyone craves. A stable MLM organization and income is nothing more than the natural result of doing the basics.

The destination - stability - is reached by deciding that it's where you want to be, and committing to get there. It's that basic, yet, most people never decide where to go. And the trouble with not having any goals is that you can run up and down the field all your life without ever scoring.

So, if stability is where you want to be, acknowledge it now, and make a long-term commitment to getting there. The track is now laid and will be wrapped up in a nice, neat package in the next chapter.

STEP 6 IS LONG-TERM GOAL AND COMMITMENT (PURPOSE)

My signature below is proof positive that I want to have a stable MLM organization, generating a long-term monthly

income amounting to at least $ _____ . I commit to being the source of this organization and to building it

to this point by _____ , 19 ____ , realizing that I must never lose sight of the basics.

Furthermore, the following is what I consider my noble purpose in life:

_____

_____

_____

_____

_____

_____

_____

_____

_____

MY SIGNATURE _____

ANNUAL REUNIONS

A final point to consider, once your organization becomes sizable and stable, is to sponsor annual "family reunions." These annual events offer the participants the opportunity to combine business with pleasure. The event offers fellowship, training, inspiration, and a tax-deductible vacation. It might be held at a convention hotel, a resort, or on a cruise ship.

If your company sponsors a national convention each year, your personal "family reunion" could be coordinated to be a part of the whole. In other words, your downline could travel together, stay in the same hotel, have meals together, and sit in the same section of the convention center, etc.

If you've just started playing the game, you needn't even consider anything in this area, other than attending your upline's reunion.

POINTS TO REMEMBER:

CONTRIBUTION MAKES
THE WORLD OF MLM GO
AROUND.

THE UNIVERSE HONORS
ALL CLEARLY DEFINED
INTENTIONS WHICH ARE
BACKED BY ABSOLUTE
COMMITMENT.

TAKE A STAND ON YOUR
LIFE WORKING AND
COLLECT EVIDENCE TO
SUPPORT IT.

THE WINNING TRACK
KEEPS YOU WINNING.
SPONSORING KEEPS
YOU ON TRACK, KEEPS
YOU IN THE REALM
OF CONTRIBUTION.

WITHOUT COMMITMENT
LIFE IS DEATH.

A GOOD IDEA IS ALWAYS
MORE SEDUCTIVE THAN
THE TRUTH.

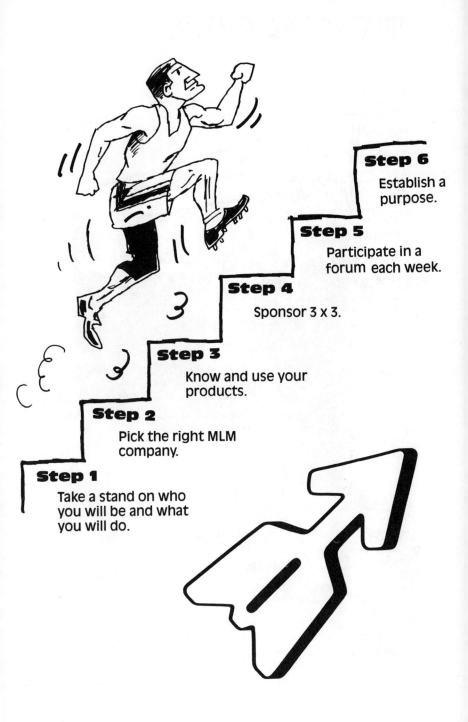

Step 6
Establish a
purpose.

Step 5
Participate in a
forum each week.

Step 4
Sponsor 3 x 3.

Step 3
Know and use your
products.

Step 2
Pick the right MLM
company.

Step 1
Take a stand on who
you will be and what
you will do.

THE SCOREBOARD

The scoreboard is where we look to see how we're doing, to see the score. In this case, our scoreboard will also help us get organized and stay that way. So the purpose of this chapter is twofold. The first is to summarize what we have committed to do (the steps). We will be able to do so in a few pages which will serve as a quick reference guide. Secondly, we're going to create a record-keeping system which will help us get our MLM business organized, and help keep it that way. People who are good time managers can get so much more accomplished with their lives, and the key to time management is being organized.

SUMMARY

MY BLUEPRINT:

At this point, we want to prioritize our goals and summarize them. In doing so, we will use the following guidelines:

1. In each category (6 mo., 1 yr., 3 yr., 6 yr., 10 yr.), rate your goals from 1 to 10, according to how they will help you accomplish your life's purpose.

2. Once prioritized, eliminate those that are "stair steps;" then list the top three in each category. An example of a "stair step" goal would be to plan a $100,000 net worth in three years, and a $1,000,000 net worth in six years. Instead of listing both in your summary, list only the top step, or six-year goal.

TEN-YEAR BLUEPRINT SUMMARY:

IN SIX MONTHS I WANT:

_____
_____
_____
_____
_____
_____
_____
_____
_____
_____
_____
_____
_____
_____
_____
_____

IN ONE YEAR I WANT:

_____
_____
_____
_____
_____
_____
_____
_____
_____
_____
_____
_____
_____
_____
_____

IN THREE YEARS I WANT:

_____
_____
_____
_____
_____
_____
_____
_____
_____
_____
_____
_____
_____
_____
_____

IN SIX YEARS I WANT:

_____
_____
_____
_____
_____
_____
_____
_____
_____
_____
_____
_____
_____
_____

IN TEN YEARS I WANT:

_____
_____
_____
_____
_____
_____
_____
_____
_____
_____
_____
_____
_____
_____
_____
_____
_____

Are you sure that you are willing to exchange the next ten years of your life for no more than what's listed above? If not, go back and design a blueprint which has a value comparable to TEN YEARS OF YOUR LIFE!

STEP ONE: MY STAND

Who I am:

_____
_____
_____
_____
_____
_____
_____
_____
_____
_____
_____
_____
_____
_____
_____
_____
_____

Who I will be:

_____
_____
_____
_____
_____
_____
_____
_____
_____
_____
_____
_____
_____
_____
_____
_____
_____

STEP TWO: MY COMPANY

My MLM company is _____ ,
and I am committed to building my organization through the channel provided
by this company. Mistakes will be made,
but as long as the company is committed
to the "grass roots" distributors, and is
doing its best, I'll be committed to it and
do my best. And above all, I will always
look for the good and never be disloyal or
even talk negatively about the company.

STEP THREE: MY PRODUCTS

I commit to an initial product purchase
amounting to $ _____ . Furthermore, I
commit to purchasing at least $ _____
worth of products each month, beginning
_____ , 19 __ . These products will be
used for samples, retail sales, and personal consumption.

STEP FOUR:
MY 39 KEY PLAYERS

Today's date is _____ , and I commit
to personally sponsor 3 and only 3 first-
level key distributors. To be considered
key distributors, they must live within
25 miles of me; they must have read this
book and made the associated commitments. I commit to having all three

sponsored by _____ (45 days
maximum).

Secondly, I commit to encouraging and
helping each of my key distributors to
sponsor 3 key distributors. I plan to have
this second generation complete with 9

distributors by _____ (90 days
maximum).

Thirdly, I commit to encouraging and
helping my first-level distributors to assist their key distributors in sponsoring
3 each. In other words, I will help spon-

sor my 27 third-level distributors by ____
(150 days maximum).

If any of the 39 distributors in these first
three generations decide not to keep
their commitments, I will replace or help
replace them. Once all 39 positions are
filled with key players, it will be appropriate for me to sponsor my second set of
3 first-level distributors.

STEP FIVE: MY FORUM PARTICIPATION

I commit to participate in a forum discussion every week. I consider these meetings to be "high priority" and will not allow anything other than spiritual, family, and career matters to interfere with them. I agree to host two per month, and to attend the two hosted by my sponsor.

STEP SIX: MY PURPOSE

My signature below is proof positive that I want to have a stable MLM organization, generating a long-term monthly income amounting to at least _____. I commit to being the source of this organization and to building it to this point by _____ , realizing that I must never lose sight of the basics.

Furthermore, the following is what I consider my noble purpose in life:

_____
_____
_____
_____
_____

ORGANIZATIONAL RECORDS
MY FIRST-LEVEL KEY PLAYERS:

1. _____
   NAME

   _____
   ADDRESS

   _____   _____
   HOME PHONE   WORK PHONE

2. _____
   NAME

   _____
   ADDRESS

   _____   _____
   HOME PHONE   WORK PHONE

3. _____
   NAME

   _____
   ADDRESS

   _____   _____
   HOME PHONE   WORK PHONE

MY SECOND-LEVEL KEY PLAYERS

1. _____ (_____)
   NAME   SPONSOR #

   _____
   ADDRESS

   _____   _____
   HOME PHONE   WORK PHONE

2. _____ (_____)
   NAME   SPONSOR #

   _____
   ADDRESS

   _____   _____
   HOME PHONE   WORK PHONE

3. _____ (_____)
   NAME   SPONSOR #

   _____
   ADDRESS

   _____   _____
   HOME PHONE   WORK PHONE

4. _____ (_____)
   NAME   SPONSOR #

   _____
   ADDRESS

   _____   _____
   HOME PHONE   WORK PHONE

5. _____ (_____)
   NAME   SPONSOR #

   _____
   ADDRESS

   _____   _____
   HOME PHONE   WORK PHONE

NOTE: The sponsor is the number on the previous level
which is occupied by his sponsor's name, address and
phone numbers.

6. _____ (_____)
   NAME   SPONSOR #

   _____
   ADDRESS

   _____   _____
   HOME PHONE   WORK PHONE

7. _____ (_____)
   NAME   SPONSOR #

   _____
   ADDRESS

   _____   _____
   HOME PHONE   WORK PHONE

8. _____ (_____)
   NAME   SPONSOR #

   _____
   ADDRESS

   _____   _____
   HOME PHONE   WORK PHONE

9. _____ (_____)
   NAME   SPONSOR #

   _____
   ADDRESS

   _____   _____
   HOME PHONE   WORK PHONE

MY THIRD-LEVEL KEY PLAYERS

1. _____ (_____)
   NAME   SPONSOR #

   _____
   ADDRESS

   _____   _____
   HOME PHONE   WORK PHONE

2. _____ (_____)
   NAME   SPONSOR #

   _____
   ADDRESS

   _____   _____
   HOME PHONE   WORK PHONE

3. _____ (_____)
   NAME   SPONSOR #

   _____
   ADDRESS

   _____   _____
   HOME PHONE   WORK PHONE

4. _____ (_____)
   NAME   SPONSOR #

   _____
   ADDRESS

   _____   _____
   HOME PHONE   WORK PHONE

5. _____ (_____)
   NAME   SPONSOR #

   _____
   ADDRESS

   _____   _____
   HOME PHONE   WORK PHONE

6. _____ (_____)
   NAME   SPONSOR #

   _____
   ADDRESS

   _____   _____
   HOME PHONE   WORK PHONE

7. _____ (_____)
   NAME   SPONSOR #

   _____
   ADDRESS

   _____   _____
   HOME PHONE   WORK PHONE

8. _____ (_____)
   NAME   SPONSOR #

   _____
   ADDRESS

   _____   _____
   HOME PHONE   WORK PHONE

9. _____ (_____)
   NAME   SPONSOR #

   _____
   ADDRESS

   _____   _____
   HOME PHONE   WORK PHONE

10. _____ (_____)
    NAME   SPONSOR #

    _____
    ADDRESS

    _____   _____
    HOME PHONE   WORK PHONE

11. _____ (_____)
    NAME   SPONSOR #

    _____
    ADDRESS

    _____   _____
    HOME PHONE   WORK PHONE

12. _____ (_____)
NAME   SPONSOR #

_____
ADDRESS

_____   _____
HOME PHONE   WORK PHONE

13. _____ (_____)
NAME   SPONSOR #

_____
ADDRESS

_____   _____
HOME PHONE   WORK PHONE

14. _____ (_____)
NAME   SPONSOR #

_____
ADDRESS

_____   _____
HOME PHONE   WORK PHONE

15. _____ (_____)
NAME   SPONSOR #

_____
ADDRESS

_____   _____
HOME PHONE   WORK PHONE

16. _____ (_____)
NAME   SPONSOR #

_____
ADDRESS

_____   _____
HOME PHONE   WORK PHONE

17. _____ (_____)
    NAME   SPONSOR #

    _____
    ADDRESS

    _____   _____
    HOME PHONE   WORK PHONE

18. _____ (_____)
    NAME   SPONSOR #

    _____
    ADDRESS

    _____   _____
    HOME PHONE   WORK PHONE

19. _____ (_____)
    NAME   SPONSOR #

    _____
    ADDRESS

    _____   _____
    HOME PHONE   WORK PHONE

20. _____ (_____)
    NAME   SPONSOR #

    _____
    ADDRESS

    _____   _____
    HOME PHONE   WORK PHONE

21. _____ (_____)
    NAME   SPONSOR #

    _____
    ADDRESS

    _____   _____
    HOME PHONE   WORK PHONE

22. _____ (_____)
    NAME   SPONSOR #

    _____
    ADDRESS

    _____   _____
    HOME PHONE   WORK PHONE

23. _____ (_____)
    NAME   SPONSOR #

    _____
    ADDRESS

    _____   _____
    HOME PHONE   WORK PHONE

24. _____ (_____)
    NAME   SPONSOR #

    _____
    ADDRESS

    _____   _____
    HOME PHONE   WORK PHONE

25. _____ (_____)
    NAME   SPONSOR #

    _____
    ADDRESS

    _____   _____
    HOME PHONE   WORK PHONE

26. _____ (_____)
    NAME   SPONSOR #

    _____
    ADDRESS

    _____   _____
    HOME PHONE   WORK PHONE

27. _____ (_____)
    NAME   SPONSOR #

    _____
    ADDRESS

    _____   _____
    HOME PHONE   WORK PHONE

MAILING LIST

The mailing list was mentioned in Chapter Four, but it needs emphasizing. We suggest that you keep a set of labeled envelopes so that when a communiqué is necessary, all you have to do is make copies of the letter and stuff them in the pre-addressed envelopes. If you're not familiar with the 33 per page, letter size sheets of labels, you might check your office supply for Avery Labels, Number 5351. If it's not apparent how to use them, just ask the sales clerk for an explanation.

PHONE TREE

If everyone does his part, the phone tree can move a message downline quickly. The phone tree works by you calling your three first-level, who call their three first-level, who call their three first-level, etc. It will work efficiently, every time, if each distributor follows through. And to follow through means that if you can't reach one of your first-level distributors, you call his three for him, etc. There will be times when you will want to communicate the same message by phone, as well as, by mail.

The need for timely and effective communication cannot be overemphasized. In the past, I considered myself to be independent, self-sufficient, and a survivor. But what I've come to realize is that we do not exist as individuals. We are relationships! Therefore, in order for relationships to work, our communication must work. And for our communication to work, it must not only be timely, but it must come from contribution.

The truth of the matter is that without contribution, there is no communication. When we come from contribution, our communication creates space for others to show up as contribution.

In thinking about the interrelatedness of contribution and communication last weekend, I coined the word "contrunicate." It combines the words contribute and communicate, and, for me, expresses the fact that to contribute is communication, and that anything less is unempowering and often damaging to others.

So, let's be in regular "contrunication" with our downline family and let's make a big difference in their lives.

HANGING FILES

Personally, I have found that a legal size file cabinet, with hanging file folders, is a simple, efficient way to organize an incredible amount of forms, literature, records, etc. Again, your office supply can show you how to set up the system. Following are some suggested file names:

ACCOUNTING:	DOWNLINE RECORDS:	MISCELLANEOUS
Cash Receipts	First-Level Distributors	RECORDS:
Accounts Payable	Second-Level Distributors	Brochures
Accounts Paid By Check	Third-Level Distributors	Coaches' Corner
Bank Deposits	Mailing List	Distributor Applications
Bank Statements	Letters & Newsletters	Forum Outlines
Bank Supplies		Letterheads & Envelopes
Product Purchases		Literature Order Forms
Product Sales		Magazines
Bonus Statements		Product Order Forms
Literature Purchases		
Literature Sales		

VOLUME AND BONUS RECORDS

Month	Personal Volume	Downline Volume	Bonus Amount	Accumulated Bonus
1.				
2.				
3.				
4.				
5.				
6.				
7.				
8.				
9.				
10.				
11.				
12.				
13.				
14.				
15.				

VOLUME AND BONUS RECORDS

Month	Personal Volume	Downline Volume	Bonus Amount	Accumulated Bonus
16.				
17.				
18.				
19.				
20.				
21.				
22.				
23.				
24.				
25.				
26.				
27.				
28.				
29.				
30.				
31.				

POINTS TO REMEMBER:

SCOREBOARD

* **BLUEPRINT**
* **MLM COMPANY**
* **MLM PRODUCTS**
* **39KEY PLAYERS**
* **BIMONTHLY FORUMS**
* **PURPOSE**
* **ORGANIZATIONAL RECORDS**
* **MAILING LIST**
* **PHONE TREE**
* **HANGING FILES**
* **VOLUME & BONUS RECORDS**

The scoreboard is how we keep track of how we are doing. Precise record keeping is a must!

KEEP SCORE!
ORGANIZE YOUR RECORDS

FINANICIAL INDEPENDENCE

THE NEW ERA IN MULTI-LEVEL MARKETING

As the shift from survival to contribution begins to take place in multi-level marketing, there will be a shift in the image of multi-level and a shift in people's attitudes toward it. The current image of MLM is that of a business within which there has been a lot of mischief. In most instances, it lacks the image of professionalism. But you, our downlines, and I are in the process of changing all that. As more and more distributors share the principles of WINNING THE GREATEST GAME OF ALL, MLM will become recognized for what it really is, a "rapid transit" vehicle through which we can make a real difference in the lives of individuals and, ultimately, the world.

Ken Keyes wrote a book called THE 100TH MONKEY in which he recorded the findings of a scientific expedition. The expedition was a large one, sponsored by the National Geographic Society, and they witnessed what has been named the Critical Mass Theory. This phenomena is unexplainable by ordinary scientific methods, yet it works throughout life, and it will help usher in the new era of multi-level marketing.

In order to clarify the Critical Mass Theory, we'll take a look at how it was discovered.

The time frame was 1952 to 1958; the place was a number of islands in the South Pacific; the characters were a group of scientists; and the purpose was to observe and record the characteristics and habits of the local plant and animal life.

The monkeys who inhabited the islands were of particular interest. The scientists would give them names and record their activities in a diary. The monkeys' main food source was sweet potatoes, which the scientists would scatter on the ground. They liked the taste of the raw potatoes, but found the dirt unpleasant.

On the island of Koshima, a young female monkey named Imo found that she could solve the problem by washing the potatoes in a nearby stream. She taught this trick to her mother and her playmates, who also taught their mothers. This cultural innovation was gradually picked up by various monkeys. During the six-year period many of the Koshima monkeys learned to wash sweet potatoes in order to make them more palatable. But it was only the adult monkeys who imitated their children that learned this social improvement.

In the autumn of 1958 something startling took place; a breakthrough, a new era began. When the phenomena took place, the exact number of monkeys who had learned to wash their sweet potatoes was unknown. But one morning, when that number reached a certain point, let's say 100, it happened. By that evening almost every monkey in the tribe was washing its sweet potatoes.

The added energy of this 100th monkey somehow created an ideological breakthrough. Yet, the most surprising thing noticed by the scientists was that the habit of washing sweet potatoes suddenly and spontaneously jumped over the sea. Colonies of monkeys on other islands, and mainland troops of monkeys, began washing their sweet potatoes.

Thus, when a certain critical number achieve awareness, this new awareness can be communicated from mind to mind. Although the exact number may vary, the 100th monkey phenomenon means that when a limited number of people know of a new way, a point is reached where only one more person needs to tune into the new awareness to cause it to reach almost everyone else.

The group dynamics of extrasensory communication can be amplified to a powerfully effective level when the consciousness of the hundredth monkey is added. Your awareness is needed to usher in the new era of multi-level marketing. You may be the hundredth person. You may furnish the added consciousness energy necessary to create the image of multi-level marketing as an industry based upon contribution.

The real power of WINNING THE GREATEST GAME OF ALL, and the reason it can initiate the new era of MLM, is that it is not a "how to" book. It is not just another technique or good idea. It is a shift, a shift from survival to contribution, and as such, it is truly a breakthrough.

The following questions might help clarify: How many books on leadership would you have to read for it to have an impact on your ability to lead? How many MLM success stories would you have to read for it to have an impact on your ability to be a MLM success? I say that there won't be much of an impact, no matter how many you read!

To improve your ability you must play the game. You see, the reason the "how to's," the techniques, the rituals don't work is because it's not the understanding but the doing which produces results. You already know everything you need to know, you have everything you need to have, you can do everything you need to do, and you are everything you need to be in order to experience MLM success. You don't need someone else's style or technique. You need only to be you. The secret is to play; to play full-out. You have the ability to be human and to contribute to other humans. Your natural, "God given" talents need merely to be channeled in the right direction. And that's the purpose of WINNING THE GREATEST GAME OF ALL.

When you play the game according to WINNING THE GREATEST GAME OF ALL, you play with power. Your power comes as a result of defined intentions pursued committedly. Your natural abilities are focused on specific results. You know exactly what to do and when to do it - no guessing, no going off on tangents, no spinning your wheels.

Life is thrilling, and accelerated life is even more so! And by the way, life is problems, and accelerated life is even more so! If your life is about trying to avoid or eliminate problems, if you think it's not okay to have problems, then you are in for a life of misery. Don't allow yourself to get caught up in the fantasy that it's possible to not have problems. LIFE IS ABOUT PROBLEMS! The most successful and noble people throughout history lived and achieved in the face of problems. Their power came from accepting responsibility for their lives. Accepting that you are the cause of your life makes you bigger than problems and circumstances. Life remains just as risky, but you have the power to deal with it. If you want WINNING THE GREATEST GAME OF ALL to eliminate your problems, you are going to be greatly disappointed. It's true, this book does coach you through many areas where distributors get stuck, but problems exist and always will.

Problems or not, it's exciting for me to share life with someone as magnificent as you. And it's even more exciting to have a game to play with you. MLM is a great game! It wouldn't be the same without you, and it will never be the same with you.

Why? Because you are committed, you play by the rules, you're a good sport, and you play full-out, in such a way that it makes a difference for all of us.

Thanks! See you at the "Victory Party."

POINTS TO REMEMBER:

This is a new era for MLM.

WINNING THE GREATEST GAME OF ALL is not a "how to" book. You already knew how to. It is a track leading to the desired destination.

WHAT WE ARE AND DO filters down through our organization. Be rigorous about your commitment, product usage and integrity. Rigorous upline integrity creates space for downline integrity, and organizational integrity is vital. In the past, we have seen distributors discredit themselves and damage their organizational integrity by dishonoring copyright laws. You will want to caution your downline to honor ours if they are going to play according to WINNING THE GREATEST GAME OF ALL. Besides, our books and tapes are priced so low that everyone can afford them. Since most new distributors will want 12 books (3 for each of their first-level and 9 for each of their second-level), our best price break is at 12 copies.

I truly hope to meet you and your MLM family. If you would like me to talk to your group, please contact me through:

CIMARRON MANAGEMENT
CORPORATION
1001 Terlton Road
Jennings, Oklahoma 74038
(918) 757-2212

Cordially,

Randy J. Ward

Randy J. Ward

PLAY AND WIN!

...THE ACCELERATED GAME OF LIFE!

APPENDIX

HOW TO RECEIVE ONGOING SUPPORT . . .
T.N.T. TOTAL NETWORK TRAINING
"A Guide to Explosive Growth"

This is not the end of this book and your coaching. Actually, we've only just begun. Our relationship can be mutually empowering for many years to come. As a student of our Total Network Training (T.N.T.), you will receive coaching and support on an ongoing basis. The Training Topics will empower you and coach you on how to train your downline.

Once you understand the rules and have formulated a game plan, coaching becomes a key factor in your success. Even the most successful players require coaching. And, in actuality, the high-performers are usually those who are the most coachable.

Each topic in the Training Program presents you with a power-packed play. And each play will be another piece to the puzzle of "what works in life." But more importantly, each topic is a new play to teach your team at the forum meetings. This systematic coaching continues to fan your natural motivational fire. It might be just the ingredient to turn it into a roaring blaze.

The Training Program consists of: a clothbound version of this book, six cassette tapes, a three-ring binder, and twelve training topics. One of the cassette tapes has been called, "the best recruiting tape ever produced for network marketing." Following are titles of some of the Training Topics:

TRANSFORM LIVES THROUGH
   ACKNOWLEDGEMENT!
HOW TO HAVE POWER WITH PEOPLE!
IN SEARCH OF THE IDEAL BUSINESS!
TO DREAM OR NOT TO DREAM?
THE WISDOM OF THE AGES!
SEVEN STEPS TO A LIFE THAT WORKS!

We invite you to play MLM by the rules set forth in WINNING THE GREATEST GAME OF ALL, and we invite you to purchase the T.N.T. Program. It will support you and help you empower your downline. And, it will be worth much more to you than what it costs.

"THE NETWORKER" SOFTWARE

If you have an IBM Compatible Computer, you can computerize and **track your downline with ease.**

1. **Keep your "Family Tree" in order.**

2. **Generate mailing labels,** or print names and addresses on individual (preprinted) letters. Just fold and stuff them in a window envelope.

3. **Generate a list of your complete downline** Alphabetically, in Zip Code order, by Social Security numbers, or in Family Tree order.

4. The Networker **can be customized** and is expandable to include Order Processing, Inventory Control, Sales Tax Accounting, Commissioning and Check Writing, annual Income Tax Reports, etc.

Whether you're merely a Distributor, or an aspiring MLM Company owner, **The Networker will take you from where you are now, to where you want to be!**

Call 800-324-2266 and order yours today!

Only $79.95!

Do you need 3 1/2" or 5 1/4" floppy disks?

ABOUT THE AUTHOR

Randy Ward, by the age of 37, has experienced success in a variety of areas. He worked his way through college as a top ten salesman for the Southwestern Publishing Company of Nashville, Tennessee. During college he became a private pilot and currently holds a commercial pilot's certificate with an instrument rating.

His first business venture beyond college was to write more than three million dollars worth of life insurance in two years. But his rapid advancement toward financial independence began when he became a real estate broker and started his own company in 1976. Between 1976 and 1980, he bought, sold and constructed dozens of houses and developed over 2,000 acres of raw land into homesites. Then in 1980, Randy became an oil producer and drilled 21 wells before entering multi-level marketing in the spring of 1983. His first year's group volume exceeded a million dollars.

Randy's diversified past has convinced him that the most rewarding way to achieve financial independence is through owning a business. As the owner of several companies, he has come to realize that multi-level marketing is the businessman's business. It can be started on a shoestring, requires no employees, very little inventory and only basic accounting. Yet multi-level marketing offers the greatest of rewards, because it is a people business. Randy calls multi-level marketing "the accelerated game of life," because it speeds up the process of personal growth and is a very direct path to friends, self-expression, wealth, travel and making a contribution in life. He sees multi-level marketing as a game, you as a player and coach, and this book as your guide. It is a handbook which defines the game, explains the rules, tells you what to expect, outlines a proven game plan, and gives you a scoreboard with which to monitor your progress.

Randy considers multi-level marketing a vehicle through which lives can be transformed, a vehicle through which we can make a great and powerful contribution to others. Read WINNING THE GREATEST GAME OF ALL and you will be able to make a quality decision as to whether you want to play or merely be a spectator in "the accelerated game of life." And if you decide to play, you will do so with focus and commitment, you will play full-out, and you will make a difference. And it is players like you who will help usher in what Randy calls the new era in multi-level marketing.

Currently, Randy is involved in "the leading edge" of progress in multi-level marketing. He is a consultant, trainer, and motivator. He has designed marketing plans and business strategies for several progressive companies.

CMC / WFP
CIMARRON MANAGEMENT CORPORATION
WARD FAMILY PARTNERSHIP

ORDER FORM

333 American Way, Jennings, OK 74038-0158   (918) 757-2235 or 757-2212

Purchaser	Date
Address	Phone
City	State Zip
CARD TYPE #	EXP

PRODUCT DESCRIPTION	QTY. ORD.	UNIT COST	TOTAL	
WINNING THE GREATEST GAME OF ALL (84 PAPERBACK books per case)		9.95		
WINNING THE GREATEST GAME OF ALL CLOTHBOUND BOOK		14.95		
WINNING THE GREATEST GAME OF ALL 1 Hour AUDIO CASSETTE TAPE		9.95		
SELLING - RECRUITING - MANAGING (64 books per case)		11.95		
90 Minute VIDEO TRAINING "What Makes the Difference?"		19.95		
T.N.T. - TOTAL NETWORK TRAINING Cassette Study Course		79.95		
"THE NETWORKER" Downline Tracking Software (IBM)		79.95		

DISCOUNTS:				
4 - 11 COPIES = 30%		TOTAL		
12 - 23 COPIES = 40%				
24 - 1 CASE = 50%		SHIPPING $4 MIN.		
1 - 4 CASES = 65%				
5 - 9 CASES = 70%		GRAND TOTAL		
10 CASES + = 75%				

CMC / WFP
CIMARRON MANAGEMENT CORPORATION
WARD FAMILY PARTNERSHIP

ORDER FORM

333 American Way, Jennings, OK 74038-0158   (918) 757-2235 or 757-2212

Purchaser_____ Date_____

Address_____ Phone_____

City_____ State_____ Zip_____

CARD TYPE_____ #_____ EXP_____

PRODUCT DESCRIPTION	QTY. ORD.	UNIT COST	TOTAL	
WINNING THE GREATEST GAME OF ALL (84 PAPERBACK books per case)		9.95		
WINNING THE GREATEST GAME OF ALL CLOTHBOUND BOOK		14.95		
WINNING THE GREATEST GAME OF ALL 1 Hour AUDIO CASSETTE TAPE		9.95		
SELLING - RECRUITING - MANAGING (64 books per case)		11.95		
90 Minute VIDEO TRAINING "What Makes the Difference?"		19.95		
T.N.T. - TOTAL NETWORK TRAINING Cassette Study Course		79.95		
"THE NETWORKER" Downline Tracking Software (IBM)		79.95		

DISCOUNTS:

4 - 11 COPIES	=	30%
12 - 23 COPIES	=	40%
24 - 1 CASE	=	50%
1 - 4 CASES	=	65%
5 - 9 CASES	=	70%
10 CASES +	=	75%

TOTAL

SHIPPING $4 MIN.

GRAND TOTAL